BE THE BETTER BROKER

VOLUME 1:

BECOME A TOP PRODUCER:
A STUDY OF MORTGAGE AGENTS,
ORIGINATORS & LOAN OFFICERS

DUSTAN WOODHOUSE

PRAISE FOR BE THE BETTER BROKER

The Amazon (both .ca and .com) Reviews are in...

83 Five Star Reviews for **Volume 1** ...and counting
59 Five Star Reviews for **Volume 2** ...and counting
24 Five Star Reviews for **Volume 3** ...and counting

Please post a review of your own, and email a copy direct to *dustan@ourmortgageexpert.com* to receive a bonus chapter as a thank you.

Volume 1

INSPIRING AND CRITICALLY INFORMATIVE!
By Ron van Someren on May 23, 2017
★ ★ ★ ★ ★

Great read. I just honestly felt like I was sitting down and having coffee with the author as he gave some incredible insight and tips on becoming a mortgage broker. He also references some other incredible books, websites and videos that he credits that I also found extremely useful. Very good read. I am certainly going to be picking up his other books.

I AM NOW A BETTER BROKER
By Brad Lockey on March 15, 2017
★ ★ ★ ★ ★

Thank you Dustan for the clarity and candidness of your thought processes. I am definitely better off after reading your series.

I HAVE BEEN IN THE MORTGAGE INDUSTRY FOR OVER 15 ...

By Calum Ross on April 5, 2017

I have been in the mortgage industry for over 15 years and been investing in courses to help my improve my client process and customer service since day one. I really wish these books had existed when I first started as they would have put me light years ahead a lot sooner. This is a must read for anyone who wants to build a meaningful client centred profitable business in the industry.

GREAT REFERENCE TOOL. CONCISE READ. HE PRACTICES WHAT HE PREACHES.

By Amazon Customer on April 19, 2017

I just finished reading volume one. As a new broker, it was an easy read that does not make too many tasks to focus on and makes getting started achievable. Dustan provides great tactics and I will definitely be using this book as a reference tool and will be reading it again.

I am truly motivated between the support of my brokerage and the series and I'm looking forward to reading volume 2 and 3.

GREAT FOR NEW BROKERS—MAYBE SHOULD BE ADDED TO THE MORTGAGE LICENSING COURSE IN ONTARIO!

By Amazon Customer on November 5, 2015

Thank you Dustan! Finally, someone has written a book about starting out as a broker in Canada. Our market is a bit different then the U.S.

This gives you great insight into becoming a Mortgage Agent in Canada. 80 hour weeks! Dustan lays it out clearly and honestly. It is a great read from start to finish. Two things standout - 1. Dustan tracks everything, stays in touch, and is out there - 90% retention rate - wow. 2. Contact Cards - again - vital to staying in touch and keeping a database. It shows you that it is vital to have and use certain tools such as Excel, CRM and different apps that are available today....You must spend a bit to get set up but where can you get into a business for 2 or 3000 dollars with the potential to earn more than a doctor or lawyer...This is a business where you are always learning.

BUY A BOX!
By Jay Seabrook on November 13, 2015

A first class read written by someone who truly walks the talk and who also learned each of these valuable lessons hands on.

If you're considering being a Broker of any kind, this book is an absolute must read. All Brokerage Owners, Managers and Mentors should really read this and consider purchasing a box to hand to everyone who is looking to join your team.

Psyched about Volume 2 and 3!

AND THIS BOOK COULD NOT HAVE COME AT A BETTER TIME FOR ME
By Sara Lussier on September 27, 2015

I have been licensed as a broker for 6 months now, and this book could not have come at a better time for me. Be The Better Broker is jam packed with information about how to grow my business, and how to do so efficiently. This book includes marketing ideas, books to read, and tech gadgets that will lead me to a successful career in mortgage brokering. I highly recommend this book, and I am looking forward to reading volume number two.

TOP MORTGAGE BROKER SHARES HIS SECRETS FOR SUCCESS
By Ross Taylor on October 11, 2015

Who would have thought a niche topic like becoming a better mortgage broker has the potential to be a best seller? Yet, I have no doubt that is exactly what Dustan Woodhouse has created here. I envision most major Canadian mortgage brokerage firms making this series of books required reading for all aspiring mortgage brokers.

In fact, I only have one 'complaint', and that is I wish Dustan had already written volumes two and three of this captivating series.

There are so many takeaways from this book, it is hard to come up with a list of the highlights. But for me, they are as follows: Chapter 4 is called "Three things we wish we had known". Here Dustan asks twenty one brokers to identify the top three things they wish they had been told before taking the course, let alone entering the business.

A recurring theme from this chapter; indeed throughout the book, is that our industry is generally woeful when it comes to preparing newbies to be successful in the real world of mortgage brokering. With respect, the licensing course is a formality, and does nothing to ensure success in the real world.

Mentoring is hugely important, yet is rarely seen and done. Dustan laments "the fact is that currently the industry lacks robust training."

The bulk of volume 1 is mostly about Dustan's tenets for personal success. He generously shares all the little things he does routinely which collectively add up to make him a super-focused, highly disciplined sales machine. He might object to this characterization, as he repeatedly emphasizes it's all about doing the right thing for the client, and success will follow.

It's not necessary to replicate everything Dustan does – some of it may not feel comfortable or natural. But clearly he is not simply stumbling along in his pursuit of greatness – he has a plan, a vision of who he is, and how he wishes to be perceived, and his actions and approach to his business are all consistent with this.

Another recurring theme is about self-discipline – in today's techno world, so many of us allow ourselves to be distracted throughout our day. Twelve hours at work may actually only translate to a few hours of productivity. Personally I feel this is a societal problem – certainly not limited to mortgage brokers. Dustan has mastered his own domain, and he is correct it is a huge area for improvement for practically all of us.

I came into the industry a few years before Dustan, yet his achievements make my own pale in comparison. However,

I feel inspired by his writing and sincerely cannot wait to channel the knowledge he plans to share in volumes two and three.

LOVE HIS DEDICATION

By Gary on October 2, 2015

Dustan's truly a professional! He's put in way more than the 10,000 hours commonly need to Master an area of business. Love his dedication, and his devotion to his clients and the effort he puts in to his business. In business, it's all about adding value to the public and he's clearly done this with this book!

BE THE BETTER BROKER

VOLUME 1: SO, YOU WANT TO BE A BROKER?

*A primer of hard truths, hard facts, and the
hard work that comprises entry into a field
which can be as personally rewarding as it
can be devastating to the unprepared.*

ISBN 978-1-61961-350-8

Printed in Canada

Thank you!

WHAT DOES A BROKER DO?

Jonathan Ive, CDO Apple Inc. unknowingly
answered this question for us:

*"We try to solve very complicated
problems without letting people know
how complicated the problem was."*

WHAT DOES IT TAKE TO FIND SUCCESS?

"Watch your thoughts, they become words;
watch your words, they become actions;
watch your actions, they become habits;
watch your habits, they become character;
watch your character, for it becomes your destiny."

— FRANK OUTLAW

Writing a book can be a lonely job, as can writing mortgages.

There is social element involved in both processes, but at the end of the day when one finds themselves sitting at their desk at 2am or 5am, hours after all have left, or hours prior to anybody arriving, this is when one discovers the ability to breed fortitude from solitude.

I have never felt alone while writing, even in the wee hours (while alone). Instead I have an unwavering sense of support for all my endeavours through the love and optimism of my wife Kerry, daughter Hayley, and son Adam, my extended (and very tolerant) family, and a wonderful circle of friends.

The absolute backing of those around me has consistently allowed me to flourish in whatever the pursuit.

I love you all dearly,

DUSTAN

CONTENTS

2:30AM

"When you stop chasing the wrong things you give the right things a chance to catch you."

— LOLLY DASKAL

Friday, November 16, 2007, 2:30am—Tossing and turning in bed. Even with a wonderful corporate job that would be the envy of many, I was not content. I got out of bed, slipped quietly down the stairs and flipped on the computer. In the glow of the screen, I typed in my credit card number and submitted my registration for the Mortgage Brokering course. It was done; I was committed. I padded back upstairs and had the first good night's sleep in a very long time. Nearly three years after the sale of my previous business, I had finally made a decision to take control once again.

ORIGIN STORY
'LITE VERSION'

From age 17 through 34, I was consistently in the right place at the right time. Riding an import car-tuning culture wave, I grew my first business from $30,000 per year out of my parents' garage (thanks again, Mom & Dad) to a $4,000,000-per-year corporation with a fantastic partner, 14 employees and what would eventually become a series of costly, yet valuable, life lessons including, but not limited to "avoid a $100,000-per-month fixed overhead." It was an educational, wild and reasonably profitable ride for the first 15 years. And then it became all-education-all-the-time, and not the kind one seeks out. No more profits, just losses...and lessons.

During 2004, finding ourselves in a currency conversion vice, we closed off the fiscal year strong on paper, if not in reality, and found a buyer for the significant brand equity we had built.

Although not at a significant enough sale price to mitigate the personal debts incurred while funding the company during 2003 and 2004.

There had been a tectonic shift, not just with the currencies, but also within the entire import automotive performance parts industry.

I was now in the wrong place at the wrong time.

At this point in my life all I knew professionally were things automotive, and even in this I had no formal education, training, or certification.

I outlined strict criteria for the next business:

- Insulation from currency swings.
- Limited inventory requirements, ideally none.
- No long-term leases for premises.
- No requirement for staffing beyond one or two.
- No significant equipment leases.
- No onerous supplier contracts.
- Mass appeal, not another razor-thin niche.
- A "happy-client" business.

Not many businesses tick all these boxes.

In 2006, two years of searching later, fiscal realities forced a decision. I accepted a comfortable corporate job, at $62,000 per year, with a multinational corporation selling building materials. I was on the road in a nice company car, taking clients to lunches and theoretically out to play golf.[1] It was the prototypical corporate job. But I am not a golfer and was growing bored rapidly. I had been accustomed to spending 80 hours a week building something special; I needed to find that challenge once again.

For several years I had been told to look at Brokering, by my wife, close friends and even my former business partner. In the summer of 2007 when the then vice-president of one of Canada's largest Mortgage Brokerages said, within a few minutes of our meeting randomly, "you should be a Mortgage Broker,"[2] I finally took heed. I was ready.

In my first six months, I completed 13 mortgage transactions representing $8.6 million in volume. I reinvested 20% of my earnings into myself via real estate-related seminars, related industry memberships, conferences and books.

In 2009, my first full year, I completed 95 transactions, $35 million in volume. Although I didn't realize anything special was happening at first, the business was actually taking off like a rocket. I assumed every Broker was just as busy. I was wrong.

By April 2010, I could no longer operate as a one-man band. I desperately needed help and was introduced to the ultimate assistant whom I work with to this day, a truly amazing and

---

1   To this day I abhor golf. Some might say this is "heresy" in our industry. I say, "call me at the office where I will be closing files."

2   You will find the word Broker capitalized throughout this series. It is my cry for the industry to co-opt this word, or another as was done with Realtor.

fully licensed Broker (as all assistants should be) without whom, things would not be as they are today.

Business levelled up to a nice pace:

- 2010: 177 transactions – $74.6 million in volume
- 2011: 168 transactions – $74.1 million in volume
- 2012: 175 transactions – $79.8 million in volume
- 2013: 166 transactions – $69.1 million in volume

Then due to a variety of steps taken, all of which will be detailed in Volume 4 (due out in 2018) business levelled up another notch:

- 2014: 227 transactions - $103.2 million in volume
- 2015: 237 transactions - $111.4 million in volume
- 2016: 219 transactions - $112.8 million in volume
- 2017: Q1 on par for a repeat

I attribute this "next level" jump largely to preparing a detailed 178-slide presentation outlining how I was doing what I was doing, and then sharing it with 1,400 fellow mortgage agents nationwide.

Sharing with industry peers forced close scrutiny of systems and processes. Weaknesses become clear as the reality of getting up in front of 1,400 other Brokers and speaking about methods used sets in. To say the least it was a transformative experience. Those presentations made me a better Broker, and sparked the creation of this series of books.

It took six years of hard work to crack $100 million in annual volume, achieving a rank of #8.5 in the Canadian Mortgage Professional list of top-producing Brokers nationwide for 2014.[3] A goal achieved thanks only to the assistance and support of dozens of people around me: a wonderful family, great friends and an amazing assistant. The network of people within the industry around me is also fantastic and I grow more indebted to them with each passing year.

I hope that part of my debt to industry players can be repaid, and paid forward, with this series of books:

Volume 1: *So you want to be a Broker?* Is a frank preview of the business of the business. A critical read for those contemplating an entry into Brokering. It is an honest account of what it takes to get yourself into the zone of profitability in what is a very challenging industry. Packed with core principles to embrace from the start, and a proven worthwhile read for those already years into the business.

The mantra of Volume 1: *"It will not be easy, but it will be worth it!"*

Volume 2: *Days 1-100 As A New Broker, Plant Seeds for Tomorrow, While Feasting Today!* Volume 2 picks up where Volume 1 left off, essentially the day after you made the decision to become a licensed Broker. This book delves into essential

---

3   During the print run of *the annual Top 75 CMP*, editors accidentally left my numbers on the cutting-room floor. They were subsequently sequenced into the online issue with a ranking of #8.5—in reality #9. I stressed to CMP staff that they not bump the other 67 Brokers' rankings; that would have truly been painful for #75 in particular.

steps in laying a foundation for long term success in the early days of your Brokering career. Preserve your capital, market strategically, build lasting relationships with clients and referral partners alike. Volume 2 is packed with dozens of process tips and lessons gleaned from the authors personal experience processing more than 1400 mortgage files, and the direct personal intake of more than 2000 applications both in person and by telephone (90% by telephone for good reason).

Whether you are brand new to the mortgage Broker business, or have been immersed in it for years, you will find value in these pages. The kind of value that leads to a greater number of files closed with a reduced amount of time invested.

The mantra of Volume 2: *"Get The Application."*

Volume 3: *The Nuts & Bolts, Scripts & Skills To Convert First Time Callers To File Complete!* This book presents a play-by-play account of the processing of a file. Starting with that very first 'what's your best rate' phone call and winding through the process to 'File Complete' and having things signed and sealed at the lawyer's office.

Packed with thousands of words of the exact scripts used during hundreds of conversation addressing application intake, overcoming objections before they even arise, to dealing effectively with the signing of commitment, compliance, and insurance documents. All the while using the process itself to build a base of referring clients, and all-out raving fans.

You will increase your funding ratio.

You will increase your overall volume.

Apply the principles and the scripts outlined in this book and the previous two and you will be on your way to building a 250 file per year business.

The mantra of Volume 3: *"File Complete."*

Volume 4: Level Up! Is the handbook for those with experience and a mature Brokering business that has plateaued at a certain volume, be it $5M, $25M or $55M per year for three years or more. Volume 4 is a deep dive into what it takes to make the leap, breakthrough limitations, and level up!

This work will be challenging, there is no easy button in Mortgage Brokering. Within great challenges there are opportunities for great rewards.

Now, let's dig into the realities of what it takes to become a Top Producer in the mortgage business.

CHAPTER 1

THE BEST TIME TO BECOME A BROKER

"What you do today can improve all your tomorrows."

– RALPH MARSTON

The best time to become a Broker is now!

Many great businesses are built in tough economic times. While others run for the exits, you may want to saunter through the entrance and take a look around. At the time of this writing, our economy is making incremental gains, yet there is no shortage of negativity from the media. In particular when it comes to reconciling a steadily rising housing market. So be it.

Whether the market is rising or falling, whether the economy is expanding or contracting, it matters not. This series of books is designed to assist you with carving out your own slice of any market and becoming a top producer.

The only economy that matters is the one between your own ears.

By the Numbers

Below are the numbers which cause me to spring from bed each morning:

TOTAL POTENTIAL MORTGAGE TRANSACTIONS IN BC
- 1M+ privately owned properties
- 50% *mortgage-free*
- 500,000 potential transactions
- Remove all purchase, refinance and equity take-out transactions
- Assume all 500,000 go for full five-year terms
- Approximately 100,000 up for renewal alone
- Assume 90% renew with their current lender
- 10,000 renewal transactions remain for you
- You need how many transactions (files) to have a solid year?
- 100 files?
  - → *0.01%*
- 50 files?
  - → *0.005%*

When you factor in the additional tens of thousands of purchase, refinance and equity take-out transactions that occur each year, the overall percentage of transactions required drops to as low as 0.001% of the market. 0.001% earns you a great living.

Take some time to research the numbers of privately owned properties in your province or state and build your own motivational worksheet.

You would be correct in pointing out the absence of a total number of Mortgage Brokers and bank mortgage reps in BC in these numbers. Nor breakdown by Broker market share. Regardless of the amount of competition (a few thousand per Province by most estimates) or the size of current Broker market share (approximately 30%), it is clear there is a massive opportunity based on just 0.001% of mortgage holders being willing to work with me, or you. Confidence is important.

Your Origin

It doesn't matter what you're currently doing for work or what you have done previously. What does matter is how you approach what you do; if you have always approached the task at hand, whatever it be, with the aim of doing it as efficiently, as thoroughly and as well as it could possibly be done, then your mindset is already on the right track. The keys to success are a willingness to learn, an optimistic outlook and hard work.

My own background included neither financial services-related jobs nor real estate industry-related work. However, whatever work has come my way, I have always attacked it with a desire to do better than it has been done before. The value in this style of working is well addressed by Robin Sharma in *The Leader Who Had No Title*.[4] Such an approach

4   *The Leader Who Had No Title*: A Modern Fable on Real Success in Business and in Life – Dec 28 2010 by Robin Sharma

allowed me within 24 months of entering the business to be ranked by Canadian Mortgage Professional (CMP) as a Top 50 Broker, and remain there consistently in the top 20—in a nationwide field of 18,000+ agents.

You've got to be the first to believe that you can be awesome. Forget about "ABC" (Always Be Closing), and embrace "ABA"—*Always Be Awesome.* ABA as a mantra will drive your progress in Brokering; it will drive you into the top 1% of the industry. Your self-belief and self-confidence will prove contagious: contagious with clients, referral sources and industry partners. The advice, insights and case studies sourced from my own rocket launch into this business and the (to date) 1200+ completed mortgage transactions will assist you in avoiding common—and uncommon—mistakes.

You will be a confident Broker. You will be an awesome Broker.

You will *Be the Better Broker.*

CHAPTER 2

OVERCOMING OBJECTIONS

"The longer you wait for the future the shorter it will be"
— AUTHOR UNKNOWN

Optimism Matters

First learn to overcome internal objections, then work on overcoming client objections. Focus on the positive side of any and all events as often as possible; turn challenges into competitive advantages. This is a worthwhile workout for the mind. It can be a great game to play with kids: How is getting stuck in this traffic jam a good thing for us? Come up with three reasons. How is this power outage a positive event? And so on.

The following passages are an analysis and implementation of what I classify as "logical optimism," something that forms a large part of my everyday thinking.

Admittedly, not every move made can be logical, nor every thought optimistic, but there is room for most of us to utilize this approach to a much larger degree. The application of logical optimism will prove fundamental not only in your communications with clients, but also with family and friends. Family and friends who may question the seemingly risky move into a career that is 100% commission based. Not to mention somewhat misunderstood.[5]

Logical optimism can be used to formulate a case for becoming a Broker specifically because you are female or male, married or divorced, have no children or have seven children, prefer to be highly social or prefer to work from home and rarely venture into social settings. The point is, nearly any perceived obstacle can be presented as a strength, or at least as an opportunity. Ryan Holiday's excellent book, *The Obstacle is the Way*,[6] makes this point.

A common refrain against making the leap into a new career, particularly Brokering, is often an age-related one. The answer to the question, "Are you the right age?" is, "Yes, the right age is whatever age you are *today*."

When an aspiring Broker believes their age is a potential

---

5   Misunderstood to be a "lender of last resort." In fact, within my role as a Mortgage Broker my clientele is more than 90% "AAA," composed of successful business owners with excellent credit, sharp intellects and often multiple properties. They are experts in their own fields and appreciate working with another expert whenever possible.

6   *The Obstacle Is the Way: The Timeless Art of Turning Trials into Triumph - Ryan Holiday.* Throughout this series, I will refer to dozens of books that have shaped much of my thinking on peak performance and on life in general. I have read each at least once, and encourage you to do the same.

obstacle to their success, it is worth visiting all the ways in which their age is actually a true advantage.

Let's apply some logical optimism; you will notice each passage begins with the same initial sentence with only the age varying. The prefix of the sentence could be reset to read just about anything you believe to be an obstacle. The more time you spend turning obstacles into pathways, the better prepared you will be for the day-to-day workings of Brokering.

Your Age Does Not Matter

At age 25, becoming a Broker could not be a better move. Your cost of living is significantly lower than for somebody who's 45 or 55. The pressure for immediate success is slightly lower. You're young, energetic and enthusiastic, and you're no doubt more tech-savvy. You may not own a house of your own, but you likely aren't married with two or three kids, a dog, two cats and a huge mortgage.

One could argue that the 25-year-old lacks life experience, meaning they'll be outshone by the 45 or 55-year-old who has more than twice the real-world experience under their belts. And while this may be true, the 25-year-old has the advantage of being significantly more fiscally nimble than the 45-year-old. They can afford to take bigger career risks as they move forward.

Factor in the number of first-time buyers in the 25-35-age bracket and clearly there are advantages to youth. If you are 25, focus on these advantages and build a list of 20 more to print out and leave on your desk. Re-read them and add more each week to boost your confidence.

At age 35, becoming a Broker could not be a better move. You have likely already bought at least one home and have a basic understanding of the mortgage process. It's possible you're married; maybe have a child or three. You have likely been through one or two careers. You may have run a business, successfully or unsuccessfully. Either way, you've got some life experience. Draw on it.

The human body reaches its peak potential in the early 30s. You're right in that zone mentally and physically, or at least should be. Physiologically your peak has not passed. Grasp this and run with it, or cycle, or swim, or lift. You've accumulated ten quality years of life experience and wisdom over the 25-year-old. Younger first-time buyers will trust you to guide them through a process you have already experienced firsthand.

Your experience also gives you credibility in the 40-something, 50-something and even 60-something minds. Clients in these demographics view you as being young enough to help them as long as they may need Brokerage services. At 35, you probably have a 20 or 25-year career ahead of you. You can market yourself to people as their mortgage agent for life.

Seven years ago, at age 36, I made a very impassioned case for how this was a wonderful age. Now at 43, my new passion pitch is for the 45-year-old.

There is a positive spin to put on youth and energy over outdated experience, just as there is one to put on seniority and decades of real-world experience over lack of life experience.

For all age groups, the barrier to entry into the world of Brokering is very low. From a time perspective, the course itself is typically less than three months. From a cost perspective, allow a thousand or two to get licensed and signed up with a Brokerage. Initial fixed costs are rarely more than a few hundred dollars a month for a Broker starting a successful business. Most of the job can be done from behind a telephone, with the location of the desk somewhat flexible as well.

Your Sex Does Not Matter

At the risk of putting my foot in my mouth, let's talk about sex, specifically, being a female within the Broker industry.

Recognizing my obvious limitations as a male, I asked a few female top producers to vet the next few paragraphs for me.

This is a profession in which gender equality really does exist. The compensation is performance based and blind to the sex of the Broker. A Broker is rewarded on the merit of their abilities. It is fair to say that, as many clients prefer to work with a woman as a man. Without question, the majority of clients prefer to work first and foremost with a competent, knowledgeable, and personable individual.

There's a lack of a glass ceiling for women in Mortgage Brokering because there is a lack of formal corporate culture, with progress dictated by only the Broker themselves, rather than a crusty layer of management. You are your own CEO, you are your own HR department, and you are your own crusty layer of management. In this business, the only one holding you back is you.

Reviewing the 2015 Canadian Mortgage Professional Top 75 statistics, 24 of the top 75 Brokers nationwide were female. That is impressive representation. Roughly 33% of the top performers in this industry are female. This suggests significant opportunity.

Real estate has long been a career in which women have an opportunity to excel in earnings potential and market recognition. I know many strong women in this business. No doubt we raise both boys and girls in a far more egalitarian manner than generations past, but Brokering is a field already strides ahead in equality. The future continues to look brighter for the younger entrants into the industry. Both female and male.

Your Previous Experience...

However, one form of discrimination does linger within our industry. It was one I was not subjected to at the time of my hire, thanks to a visionary management team (you know who you are). I refer to the outdated concept that new Brokers should only be hired if they have a certain amount of experience specifically in the banking or financial services industry.

During my interview, the policy was that every new Broker ought to have at least two years' experience in the banking sector (even working as a teller would count). This I lacked. Then, as now, the relevance of a banking background is in fact largely lost on me. People with a financial services background comprise a large part of the 47% who fail to hit the four-year license-renewal mark.

Back in 2007, when I spoke with my first manager about whether the firm would hire me, I was in the frame of mind that the meeting was purely about them interviewing me, which to some extent was accurate of course. However, I did not realize I was meant to interview them as well.

Keep this in mind when your time to interview Brokerages comes; you are the one making the difficult decision. More so than they are. You will be paying them; they will not be paying you.

More important than financial services experience is an entrepreneurial background. To be self-starting is vital in this business. Nobody's going to nudge you out of bed and tell you to go to work. There's very little accountability in this business other than looking in the mirror and telling yourself to get to work. This is of course both a blessing and a curse. Know thyself; act accordingly.

The Best Day

Whatever your age, your sex, or your previous experience, today is arguably the ideal day to initiate a career change. The key to this is establishing confidence by shaping our own story into a tale of strength with a positive spin. You must, of course, believe your own story, and it must be your own truth. Never tell a lie and you never have to recall what you said. Belief in your own positive story, belief in why this is the perfect time; how you are the perfect age, that your specific life experiences prepare you to become a top-producing Broker is the root of self-confidence.

This is a task you can work on individually, but is much better done with friends and family who see the positive in you. Focus specifically on them. Their opinions are the ones that matter.

I believed in my story, I created my own confidence. And it was confidence born from the ashes of near-complete ego destruction a few years before.

CHAPTER 3

SO YOU WANT TO BE A BROKER?

"I hear: I forget. I see: I remember. I do: I understand."

— CHINESE PROVERB

This book is about designing and building the foundation for a launch pad, one from which you will rocket forth on day one in business. Simply being "licensed" is not enough; you need to be "licensed to kill."

The License Comes First

The first step in becoming a Broker is, of course, passing your licensing exam. The license is just your ante though. Possession of it grants you legitimacy on paper, but leaves you with very limited knowledge of how the game is played. This book is designed to provide you with a $20 ante option before you step up and commit the time and money (typically $1,000) to pass the Brokering exam. This book is also meant to prepare you for the big game; a $1,000+ ante is significant, but the time and commitment to enter a new career is more significant. Just ask one of the 36% who leave the business within two years about the deeper personal costs.

Straight up: *Brokering is difficult.* The speed with which you proceed through the licensing course will be a strong indicator of your likelihood of success. If you enrol in the preparatory course and don't open a book for the first six months, that's a sign that you're probably going to struggle to pass the exam, which in turn is a sign that you will struggle to find success in the business.

My answer to people who ask me whether they should enroll in the course has typically been (and I now think of Shia LaBeouf[7]), "***Just do it.***" Now my answer will be, "Read this book first."

Don't Quit Your Day Job

The course itself is a very light-duty correspondence program in most provinces/states, requiring little more than a few days off work, if any at all, to complete. Keep your current income if you can, right up to and through the day you take the exam. You want to be certain you have passed (not

---

7   Go to YouTube and check out both the *one-minute motivational Shia LaBeouf* videos (which is my current ringtone and morning alarm tone) and *the longer version*. He makes some great points.

everybody does) and you do not want to turn off the flow of income prematurely. However, there will come a time later in our progression together where you will turn that income tap off despite a degree of uncertainty about the future.

There is no such thing as a top producing, or a truly skilled, part-time Broker with a full-time job in another field, or even in a related one. Being top quality at anything takes focus, dedication and time commitment.

The time to make a leap from your day job and make a firm and 100% focused commitment to Brokering is not upon us at this point, not even close. Keep your current income stream; the time to review that will be after you are fully licensed.

The fundamental challenge with working another job once you start Brokering is the sporadic timing of your availability that is required by clients, Realtors, appraisers, and lenders alike to process files efficiently. The experience is anything but linear and predictable. Thus your required availability must have a very wide and accessible bandwidth to work with the deadlines imposed which are often tight and numerous.

In British Columbia[8] the course itself is entirely manageable while working. You have one year to take the exam from the day you finish the final assignment in the preparatory course. After completing the 20 assignments, you have to wait at least 30 days to take the exam.

8   I refer to the Broker course only as it stands at the time of this writing. There is a major revision of the text and format of the program underway, with contributions from long-standing successful Brokers. This holds great promise.

2 assignments per week = 10 weeks, add another 30 days wait time to take the exam then wait for the grade and the official documents and very quickly the process can stretch to 6 months. Do not quit your job to take this course, there is no need and you will suffer for it.

If you register for this course, complete the assignments quickly, book the exam immediately and get it done.

My Approach

Here's an approach that worked for me. In the evenings after work I focused on knocking out one assignment every second night. I attended all available classroom sessions (offered as supplemental) from the date I enrolled right up to the week I took the exam. There was a 500-question study guide available to prepare for the 100-question multiple-choice exam. Breaking that study guide into five mock exams I then sat down at 10am for ten straight days leading up to the exam itself, which was scheduled for 10am. Day one of the mock exam runs I scored 60%. Good thing I practiced as 65% is the minimum passing grade.

I cycled through the five mock exams twice over the ten-day period. On the tenth day, less than 24 hours before I was going to write the actual exam, I scored 93.

When it finally came time to sit for the real exam, I scored 82%, a big drop from the 93% the day before in the comforts of my own home. And so began the trumpeting to any who would listen: "Hey, I'm now a licensed Broker."

This method worked for me; perhaps it will for you as well. The key is to have a method of some sort. You are entering a business that is all about systems and processes. The firmer grasp you maintain on the flow of information, the better Broker you will be

There Are No Guarantees in Life

Some prospective Brokers pay for supplemental preparatory classes led by instructors who perform surgery on the process. They disassemble the course and the exam, and reassemble it and teach it in such a way that they "guarantee" a passing grade. (The actual guarantee is that you can take their course over and over for free until you pass). You're not learning anything other than how to score at least 65% on the exam. More valuable in the long run is learning how to learn.

I don't want to come across the wrong way here, and I don't want to belittle anyone who chooses this path. But for me (and this is a theme in my life and a thread through these books) I like to work harder than may be necessary. I crave difficulty in almost everything I do. It was not about the course content, it was about finding my own way to harness the arcane data the regulator wants absorbed and regurgitated. The harder I worked the easier new things became.

The majority of top performers in the industry did not take shortcuts with the course either; rather, they applied themselves. Many of the Brokers who have taken the "guaranteed pass" path have not lasted in the business. They have found the business too difficult. They passed the exam, but failed to learn how to learn.

Brokering is difficult. Be true to yourself and realize that if you cannot buckle down and absorb the basic data yourself, if you cannot find your own path to doing this, then you are likely to have significant trouble once licensed and working on a client's application. There is no support crew who for $1,000 will guarantee you an approval for your client. Contrary to what most Brokerages will tell you, you are on your own in this business.

There are exceptions to the "sink or swim" business model that most new Brokers encounter, but they are few and far between. In most instances it boils down to a lonesome Broker (you) sitting at a desk (alone) late at night wondering how to get a client's file approved by 5pm the next day. The stress can be intense and immense.

Shortcuts rarely work. If you have a proclivity for taking the easy way out, you may want to think twice before entering this business. Brokering is often thankless. It is exceedingly demanding of time and energy, and requires continued expansion of knowledge. As for the goal posts, they don't just move wider and narrower. They move up, down, left, right, backwards, forwards. They're all over the map.

You must know your stuff. You must convince prospective clients that you know your stuff. You must be credible and reasonably sociable, meaning you've got to be likeable, trustworthy, and honest. You have to be on the client's side. It is all about the client and solutions for the client, not solutions for you.

You must be learning constantly or you won't make it. You will benefit if you like reading (non-fiction). A love of learning will love you back. You will be better able to stay on top of ever-changing policies, products and procedures. Lenders have different sets of restrictions and (often unpublished) exceptions. If you take a client's file to seven different lenders, you may be told no for seven different reasons. Working a client's file often feels like assembling a jigsaw puzzle while blindfolded with the ability to use only your thumbs.

You get halfway through a file and think you're playing Chutes and Ladders, but the next thing you know you're playing Monopoly with Chess pieces on a Backgammon board.

And here's the real kick in the pants. The preparatory course and the exam itself don't actually prepare you to work as a Broker on a client's file. The courses spend little to no time teaching you lender policies, discussing how to obtain and work with a referral source, build a client relationship, process a client's application smoothly, select the best lender or address any of the dozens of unique situations that pop up in a file, from self-employed income to credit challenges to clearly explaining down-payment documentation requirements. Many of these examples will merit individual chapters in the next volume.

There is a movement growing to create improved ongoing education courses that do address a variety of scenarios, but much like our industry itself, such efforts are largely in fledging stages.

There are a wide variety of lender objections that will collapse a file, your job as a Broker is to understand the lender's criteria before submitting your client's file. You do not have time to waste, and neither do the lenders. For instance, very few lenders will process a file for a property to be held in the name of a holding corporation, let alone an operating corporation. Many Brokers are unaware of why this is, or even the differences between the two types of corporations, and which documents to request up front. And frustratingly the preparatory course and exam address none of these 'file-specific' issues.

Setting the Bar (Low)

The regulator's mandate is ostensibly to "protect the public," not to equip Brokers with the knowledge to be skilled in the market, to take fantastic care of their clients and to have a grasp of a variety of file scenarios, let alone an understanding of which files fit with which lender. Rather, they're protecting the public from applicants with nefarious motives. Regulators check criminal and financial backgrounds of applicants seeking licenses. This makes good sense for sure. But should the public not also be protected from a Broker who may inadvertently trigger tens of thousands in needless costs for a client by placing them with the wrong lender or mortgage. All due to a lack of experience and/or product knowledge.

Further, what also seems to be missing is an answer to this question: who is protecting the Brokers from themselves?

Think of the license as a bathing suit: it keeps you legal when interacting with the public. The course teaches you how to make the suit, which fabric to select, which thread to use, and how to stitch it all together. Awesome, you now have a bathing suit. Then the regulators drop you in the middle of the ocean and tell you to swim to shore. But hang on, you have been taught nothing of swimming, and your skills with a needle and thread are of little use now. So yes, you are legal; you will avoid arrest for public nudity, fantastic.

You've got your Brokerage license so you're not going to be arrested for practicing without one. You're "good to go."

But no, you're really not. You're in over your head, literally, and the sharks are circling. Are you going to make it to shore?

Or worse, if you do go down, are you going to drag others with you? Family members dependent on your income perhaps, or a client who was ill advised to place their mortgage with a credit union despite your awareness they were going to be transferred to another province/state within two years. It seems you were unaware that credit union mortgages are in fact not portable from one province/state to another, and you forgot about that lesson on the interest rate differential penalty. Suddenly, these clients, perhaps your friends, are paying a penalty of $12,000 plus to break their $300,000 mortgage and transfer to another province/state. If these clients have been in a flat, or worse, a declining market for the two years, between the Realtor fees, the mortgage penalty and the potential CMHC fees that ate into the equity on day one, these people may have to write a cheque to complete the sale of their property, walking away with no more down payment money, and possibly a lingering debt. This is the magnitude of power that a Broker's influence and advising has.

Statistically speaking, in the province of British Columbia, you're equally as likely to wind up as shark food than not. Of the new Brokers, 85% will not renew their licenses at the two year mark. This high attrition rate stems largely from the lack of available training on the myriad of skills required to find success in this business.

Don't look to your Brokerage house to teach you what you need to know. They no longer have the budget for high-end in-depth training. The reason behind this boils down to commissions and how they're split. Twenty years ago, the split was 50/50, half for the Broker and half for the Brokerage. When I began in 2008, an opening split of 60/40 was relatively common. Today, most Brokers are getting more than 80% of the split or better.

I am a huge proponent of attending any and all industry-related events, and our industry truly puts on some excellent ones. Every Broker should be a member of both their provincial association and national associations as well. Each year I hear Brokers complain about the cost (a few hundred dollars) of membership or the cost of the conferences. Cost is a flimsy excuse. The cost for membership and attendance on an annual basis is little more than one completed file. The opportunities to meet with peers and lenders and to hear great speakers can generate far more return than one file per year. Embrace every industry opportunity.

Search *bethebetterbroker.ca/blog/* for a post titled "Conference Like A Boss" for details on how to maximize these events.

These events are all worth attending. In particular in the early years when you may feel like you cannot afford them which is ironically enough the point at which you most need every educational opportunity you can get.

With the Brokerage houses subjected to aggressive commission splits and operating with pennies on the dollar, one can view this from two angles. Brokers are getting paid more than ever. Good for them (us). But it's a bit like the Tea Party's mantra: give me less government, I'll pay fewer taxes. So we Brokers have won that battle. But now what do we do with the extra dollars in our pockets? Invest, save, or spend? Invest in yourself.

Here's the problem: people aren't that great at taking care of themselves. In days gone by, Brokerage houses had staff dedicated to mentoring and supporting new Brokers. They were there to train you, to support you. Brokerages have now been on the run as far as commission splits are concerned for a decade or more. Their revenue model is under attack and they don't have the dollars left to invest in comprehensive training.

Your Education is Your Responsibility

If you are a brand-new Broker and have signed on at a split of 80/20 or better, you need to recognize that you must be the one to invest in yourself. If you commit to invest 10 cents of every dollar you earn in bettering yourself, you will advance beyond every other Broker around you. That is a fact.

Too many of us view a commission cheque as a pay cheque. It is not a pay cheque. The commission cheque belongs to the business, an important differentiation to live by. A Broker is running a small business. This is a big mental shift for many to make. Especially those coming into Brokering from a previously held position as an employee. That commission cheque is not yours personally; it represents your business's gross sales. A business has overhead and expenses. It cannot put 100% of revenue back in the owner's pockets and still survive, let alone thrive. You have to reinvest in your business, your baby, to keep it progressing and growing.

It is up to you!

Make. It. Happen.

What About a Mentor?

Mentoring is also a challenge in our business. Recently, a newly licensed Broker asked if he might shadow me. "Absolutely not," I told him. Not because I do not want to be helpful, but because he would learn little of value considering the stage he is at in his career. I told him if we had a time machine and could go back to my first year only then would he find value.

Most successful Brokers are giving people. They're happy to talk to you about the business. But shadowing them presents a couple of problems. First is the client's privacy. I can't abide by the concept of speaking with clients on the telephone without their knowledge that somebody is sitting in on the conversation. But more important, I would never ask clients to extend their trust to a second party; they have been referred to me, not to Mr. X and me. The client certainly wouldn't agree (and I'd never ask) for another person to overhear discussions about their personal finances. It's several levels beyond having dinner in an expensive restaurant with a trainee standing over the waiter's shoulder shadowing them. It's awkward and intrusive.

More important, successful Brokers are doing different things with their now-mature business than they did in their first year. What they're doing today is of little use to a new Broker tomorrow. Shadowing is challenging and ineffective as a training method. We learn by doing, not by observing. Role-play fills this void.

If you've picked up this book, it's a good sign. Just reading this far was a filter; you clearly have a level of curiosity driving you to do the research in advance. If you decide that Brokering is for you, you will likely be successful in the business. But this book isn't the easy button. Nor is a mentor or a training program (if you can find one). It comes down to hard work— often tedious, solitary work. It requires working late nights and early mornings, perusing three different lenders' manuals and figuring out how to get your client's file approved.

Mortgage applications are like fingerprints. Every one of them is slightly different. They all have a wrinkle in them somewhere. Even the best-looking applications contain wrinkles. It may be in the client's income or the credit score of the co-applicant or the source of the down payment. Once a lender approves the client, the wrinkle may well appear with the subject property itself. There are dozens of nuances around properties that can turn lenders off.

Having a mentor even just to run file scenarios past once a week would be of significant value. This is a small ask, just one file scenario per week, but if you keep detailed notes you will build a detailed reference manual over time. One that may have your mentor calling you to remind them a thing or two.

Questionable Career-Building Advice

New Brokers are often advised not to expect to complete their first '*deal*' for six months. I have two problems with this:

Describing what will be the most important transaction in your client's life as a "*deal*" is bad form. The word "deal" is surrounded by negative connotations. Always refer to clients' mortgages as "files." You're not trying to make a "deal," you are trying to get a "file approved," or as I like to say—daily if possible—"File Complete!" This is an important distinction. Language matters. Please eliminate the word "deal" from your Brokering vocabulary.

Wait six months for your first client's file to complete? What craziness is this? Setting such low expectations is a recipe for disaster, and all too often for new Brokers the first year can only be described as a disaster on many fronts. To be in a position of power and convey an expectation this low is problematic for all involved. And all involved would be well served to study up on the psychological concept of "the anchoring effect."[9]

The anchoring effect, suggests we are routinely, if somewhat irrationally, influenced by the original information we are given; even if this original information seems extreme to one end or the other, it still sways us. We undeniably take cues from initial starting points, especially when set by an authority figure.

Let me offer this advice: you should not expect to wait six months for a file to complete. Allow me to reset the anchoring point for you: you should complete your first file within 60 days. You should have four more files set to complete by that same time. Your first year should end with a minimum of 24 "files complete," and that should double each year for the following two years.

Now, which style of anchoring do you prefer? That which has you tracking for $2,000 of income in your first six months, or that which has you tracking for more than $48,000, then $96,000 and $192,000 in year three.

Anchoring is just one of many psychological concepts worth understanding no matter what you are doing in life. It pops up again and again, and understanding how it can work both against and for you is vital to your personal and professional success.

9   *Thinking, Fast and Slow - Apr 2 2013 by Daniel Kahneman.* An excellent book that covers "the anchoring effect," among other important topics.

The more one learns about the human condition, the more they might improve their own condition.

CHAPTER 4

THREE THINGS WE WISH
WE HAD KNOWN

What follows is a crowd-sourced chapter. The question: *What are the top three things you wish you had been told before registering for the course, let alone entering this business?*

The balance of this book goes into depth preparing you to avoid pitfalls mentioned by the Brokers below. You don't want to be looking back, as much as 12 years later, asking why nobody told you to take certain steps in advance.

This industry is in its infancy. Brokers, Brokerages, and the Super Brokers alike are finding their footing and just starting to hit their stride. The fact is that currently the industry lacks robust training. This creates significant opportunity for those that can seek out knowledge on their own.

My own answers

1. You are interviewing the Brokerage as much as they are interviewing you.

2. A vast amount of time spent with clients will be time that goes (financially) unrewarded for years to come. (But the rewards will come).

3. You will learn by doing (rightly or wrongly). There is little in the way of role-playing or client simulations for new Brokers. This is because those who can be helpful are (understandably) too busy working on their own business.

Broker #2

1. Focus on creating a database and devise a marketing/communications plan (of any sort).

2. Advise all of my closer contacts that I was shifting careers and ask them to give me a shot at securing their mortgage when due or new.

3. Meet with more seasoned Brokers for "real" feedback.

Broker #3

1. Respect that it isn't as much of a team business as most corporate environments.

2. Respect the training I was given in the past as the training I did receive was less robust and more transactional.

3. This is a sink-or-swim business. I have a wife who made (makes) a salary income, which provided me (us) the support we needed while I got up and running.

Broker #4

1. The differences between what each franchise offers/offered: training, business planning, helping to establishing processes (marketing and operations).

2. The importance of networking with colleagues and other Brokers and attending conferences. I didn't think it was necessary; boy was I ever wrong.

3. All mortgages are different. There's not one scenario that is exactly the same as another.

Broker #5

1. How long it takes to get off the ground. I underestimated the amount of time that needs to be dedicated in the beginning to get started.

2. The training was not comprehensive enough to prepare me for a "real" file.

3. For me, and I'm sure for anyone else at my age (21), book smarts and learning from listening to someone speak is all we are used to. Getting as close to real-life experience and learning life lessons from simulations that cannot just

be talked about would help immensely, especially with the current deal I have going!

Broker #6

1. Not putting as much importance on the licensing exam. All I thought about while doing that course was how am I going to pass, what do I need to do to pass, what if I don't pass? Instead, I should have been thinking, this is what I'm going to do and I'll pass, but when I do I need to have this and that already set up.

2. Once I registered in the course, passing the exam was almost seen as a finish line; it should have been seen as the starting line, forcing me to look past the exam and put together more preparation earlier on in the process.

3. Who will be your mentor and how much time and access will they give you?

Broker #7

1. How long until you see your first payday...ensure access to $ while waiting.

2. How important it is to align yourself with a great team.

3. You won't be given a single lead by your parent company.

Broker #8

1. How many real deals you need to close before you realize just how many scenarios there are...and then you need to close another 100...and another.

2. The time and money commitment to implement a marketing program.

3. The waste of time and money spent on advertising. I should have been meeting people.

Broker #9

1. Be patient...but know that it's a marathon and not a sprint...

2. Plan on making nothing for 6 to 12 months. Three-quarters of new Brokers don't get much business in year one and quit. This was not my reality, but the first year was definitely tighter than I was used to in comparison to my old salary.

3. Make adjustments and turn extra or unnecessary payments OFF. Planning = sleeping at night.

Broker #10

1. A course on how to market today. Not the old dated versions, more on technology, social media, etc. The old ways don't seem to work.

2. Have an LOC put in place prior to quitting your job;

emergency coverage enough to cover 1/2 to a year that I have dipped into in slower periods and paid off three times since.

3. This business could benefit from a stronger mentorship/coaching component in the beginning. I had some, but it still felt lacking...I could have used more. Still learning on the job now.

Broker #11

1. Stay in contact with everyone (not just past clients).

2. Understand what the product cycle is and how it mathematically applies to the business.

3. Looking for new business is a waste of time; if you're doing it right, your network should be producing all of your new business for you.

I've done the above for the last three years. Before then, from 2000 to 2012, I did not. It would be insane to know the numbers I'd be running if I stayed in contact with everyone I met from 2000 to 2012.

Broker #12

1. First and foremost, this is a sales business. If you want to be successful you will have to develop your sales skills. It is a "Technical Sales Job."

2. Stay in touch with every client every month from day one and call him or her at least once a year.

3. The phone is the most powerful tool you have to grow your mortgage biz. If you have call reluctance you will need to smash through it in order to achieve big numbers.

Broker #13

1. Find a way to stay in contact with everyone.

2. If that way does not work...find another way to stay in contact with everyone.

3. If that doesn't work...McDonald's is still hiring.

Broker #14

1. Create a process and system that adds value to every client to differentiate.

2. Treat every client like your first, your last AND only client.

3. Never stop marketing to fill the funnel...not necessarily to new referral sources but also to your existing database... Oops maybe that should be no. 1: Have a database! Be a true entrepreneur and focus on working on your business as much as you work IN your business...

Broker #15

1. Find a good CRM (Client Relationship Management) and stick with it.

2. Newsletters must go out monthly and not the "canned" version. The real-you version.

3. Don't let rate shoppers guide the conversation. Find out what the client wants and needs. Ask more questions.

Broker #16

1. Something I did know and prep for; line up back-up finances ahead of time just in case; savings and a LOC ready!

2. Let your current database know in advance that you are making a change! You may pick some up sooner rather than later.

3. CRM: start with one before you think you need it!

Broker #17

1. In my first year I would deliver 800 – 1,000 refinance flyers every week and knock on every house that had a for sale/ sold sign. I would hand them my card with a rate written behind and a $2 Timmie's gift card...not the most effective but I had three kids to feed!

2. My first year I closed 5 files from door knocking and 15 or so from flyers. I wished somebody had told me to stay in contact with those people!

3. Stay in contact with past clients!

Broker #18

1. You can know everything you want about mortgages, but if you don't have a client base, you'd better be strong on the marketing side.

2. All the assurances you get from the big Brokerages that they've got the marketing all taken care of for you...doesn't bring in a single deal.

3. You need to be able to ask for the business—not easy to learn, if you're coming from a safe, employed, salaried type of job!

Broker #19

1. No one is hungrier than you! Only you can make it happen! DON'T buy into the first-year-is-a-write-off mentality.

2. If you are going to make this work, it NEEDS to be your FT job! Marketing, calls, database, more calls. Get familiar with a few lenders AND bark up referral source trees, etc. And that is just scratching the surface. You have to get out there; you have to sell yourself.

3. Perhaps the best piece of advice I have ever heard (applicable all your life in any vocation): "Position yourself as an Expert." Even when new, you will likely know more than the average prospect. Remember that!

Broker #20

1. I would never claim that my first year was a write-off. As far as income goes, it was terrible but I worked really hard, and in terms of planting some great seeds, making good contacts and getting myself out there, it was fantastic.

2. I'm now seeing the benefits of those efforts and know that it will continue to grow as long as I keep doing what I'm doing and more!

3. I'm so grateful for the support of fellow Brokers—it's invaluable!

Broker #21

1. Focus on my core value and never sell out—stand firm on your core value.

2. Never, ever, ever burn your bridges with anyone.

3. Focus on the type of customers that I want, focus on a niche market sooner and don't be a jack-of-all-trades.

As you can see, there is consistency among these answers. Be prepared to deal with lower earnings as you get started. But do not accept low earning! The lessons you learn with each passing file will help you to gain your footing.

This chapter is evidence of the growing sense of community among Brokers from coast to coast, a community willing to share and help each other. Another example being Facebook forums "Mortgage Brokers get Serious" and "I love Mortgage Brokering." We are less alone in this field than ever before.

CHAPTER 5

UNDERSTAND YOUR MOTIVATION

"Start with Why."

— SIMON SINEK[10]

Ask yourself: what motivates you? Then ask yourself what motivates you on an intrinsic level. Aside from accolades, awards, financial success (extrinsic factors), what motivates you to do things that perhaps nobody will know you have done, and that may lead to no specific tangible or immediate (extrinsic) reward? Understanding what drives you on the deepest levels is critical to recognizing, defining and communicating your own personal brand of excellence to the world. What are you about? And why?

My personal why is to become a better me. This is why I read

---

10 *Start with Why: How Great Leaders Inspire Everyone to Take Action* – Dec 27 2011 by Simon Sinek. An excellent book, one that I subsequently purchased 50 copies of (direct from the publisher) to pass out to clients and fellow Brokers.

voraciously, listen to a variety of podcasts and attend conferences related to my field of work whenever possible. I make it a point to learn something new every day; more important, I also try to share new ideas whenever possible. It has been said that the best way to learn is by teaching. This thread runs through my daily client calls and extends to my blog posts, and is ultimately leading me to write the *Be a Better Broker* series. Why am I going to these lengths? Not for financial gain, but because I know that writing this series will help clarify and improve my own thinking, and thus my actions and habits, all in an effort to become a better me. And a better Broker.[11]

My desire to improve at what I do is fueled by each encounter with clients who have had mortgages in the past, yet were poorly informed and now find themselves paying the price for their previous Broker or bank rep's lack of knowledge or effort. For instance, I've had clients who find themselves facing significant IRD (Interest Rate Differential) penalties that were never clearly explained up front, or worse still, have paid a second (CMHC) mortgage insurance premium when moving to a new property because the person they dealt with failed to key in a request to port the coverage over to the next property. These experiences tell me that not only are clients often ill-informed, the topic of mortgages is radically oversimplified (typically to "what's the best rate") by all too many of the

---

11 To dispel any illusions that might exist about my motivations being fiscal. There was no publisher interest in this project. Instead the hours and the dollars invested are my contribution. The monetary payback on the investment would no doubt be larger were it simply focused on clients. However I feel compelled to give something back to an industry that has been so good to me. I can only hope that people find value in what I am offering.

front-line staff processing transactions. We can all be better at what we do, but only if motivated to do so.

Educating clients on all of the options and pitfalls and having them happy in the long run is what motivates me.

Happy clients are repeat clients.

Happy clients are referring clients.

Many people assume that money is the main motivation for our actions. Certainly, I have been called out on this point personally based on the number of hours I work, and/or the annual mortgage volume I process. Indeed, Brokering can produce tremendous income, but not without tremendous effort. It's not an easy business in which to flourish; however, my motivation is linked to what has become my brand. *The Expert.*

Money and mortgage volume are by-products of the pursuit of excellence.

My Motivation: *Sharing my knowledge, advising clients*[12] *and helping fellow Brokers. All in the pursuit of excellence.*[13]

I've observed individuals enter this business—and shortly thereafter exit—whose sole motivation was dollars, a.k.a.

---

12 "I advise, clients instruct" a comment I once overheard and immediately adopted as policy.

13 *Mastery – Nov 13 2012 by Robert Greene.* A masterful tome on the topic of achieving excellence at one's craft. All of Mr. Greene's writings should be required reading for high school students.

solutions for themselves. This business offers power to create positive change in people's lives, clients and Brokers alike. Instead, some who enter the field see little more than the potential to have a high-end car parked on their driveway. It is understandable to make an assumption that successful Brokers are motivated by money. Yet in my experience this is a false assumption. Those who choose the pursuit of money in Brokering rarely endure and less frequently excel, while those who pursue excellence at their craft, in turn, excel.

All too many of us are unaware of what truly motivates others to make the decisions they make, and we are often a little fuzzy when challenged on just why exactly we ourselves made certain decisions. Why did we choose to buy the sort of vehicle we did, wear the sort of shoes we do or even buy our coffee wherever we do? There is an interesting series of videos by "RSA Animate" on YouTube including one titled "Drive: The surprising truth about what motivates us."[14] It is well worth a view. And there are several excellent books on the topic of motivation available.[15] [16]

Love the Game

You would be hard-pressed to find a top-performing athlete in any sport that decided as a kid he wanted a $6-million-a-year contract. So that's why he learned to love baseball or hockey

---

14 *https://www.youtube.com/watch?v=u6XAPnuFjJc* One in a series of informative videos.

15 *Drive: The Surprising Truth About What Motivates Us* – Apr 5 2011by Daniel H. Pink

16 *Predictably Irrational Revised And Expanded Edition: The Hidden Forces That Shape Our Decisions* – Apr 8 2010 by Dan Ariely.

or basketball. Few if any were driven to excel by the money. They simply loved the game so much they worked harder than everybody else around them. The money came as a by-product of that hard work. Love of the game is key.

You don't have to look far to see this play out all around us. People chasing dollar signs just don't make it as far as those chasing excellence. There needs to be an internal drive to improve one's skills, ultimately, a love of learning and the pursuit of mastery. NBA star Steve Nash holds the record for the highest foul shot percentage, just above 90%. It is said he wouldn't leave practice until he had made 100 free throws in a row. If he made the first 99 and missed the last one, he'd start over. He didn't shoot those additional 100 free throws for the money; he did it to become the best. He was dedicated to excellence. Dedicate yourself to doing the difficult.

I'm purposely avoiding the word *passion* here. Following your passion is often a dangerous thing. You don't have to look any further than the tale of my first business[17] to see how following your passion or hobby (performance cars, in my case) can lead to struggle and potential ruin. Turning your passion into a business rarely works over the long haul. (96% of businesses fail within the first ten years). A better indicator of future success than passion is skill. Cal Newport's *So Good They Can't Ignore You*[18] does an excellent job of elaborating on this concept.

---

17   The tale of my first business was largely edited out, but for those interested it will be found via a blog post @ *bethebetterbroker.ca/blog/*

18   *So Good They Can't Ignore You: Why Skills Trump Passion in the Quest for Work You Love* – Sep 18 2012 by Cal Newport.

Passion matters, a passion for excellence at your chosen craft.

No matter the task at hand, strive for excellence and the rewards will find you. Treat every day in your life as a job interview; each person you interact with has a varying degree of power to raise you up or to pass you over. You never know which people have that power today, or might tomorrow. Thus it is logical to be pleasant all of the time. Admittedly, this is easier said than done in certain circumstances.

Keep in mind that the more time you spend building up the people around you, the greater the heights that they, in turn, can assist you in reaching.

By now you are noticing that dozens of books will be referred to throughout this series; all are well worth the investment if you are heading down this path of independence. This is partly a curation of titles that will specifically help support a Broker with beginning and growing their business.

At the end of each day I often spend another 30 to 45 minutes reading on my Kindle, tuned into an audiobook, or less frequently actually holding a hardcopy of a book, all in an effort to get away from a backlit screen as part of my own ritual around falling asleep as smoothly and deeply as possible.[19]

So, if not for money, why does one choose to become a Broker? The incredible earnings potential of a profession with an exceedingly low barrier to entry cannot be ignored.

19 *Night School: Wake up to the power of sleep (2014) by Richard Wiseman*

I concede this point. In fact, I expect any Broker who reads and applies all of the skills from this book and the next to achieve a six-figure income—that should be a baseline. An income is important of course. Given that we know the earnings potential is significant, let's ensure money is neither your primary focal point, nor sole motivator.

Percentages

What we are trying to drill down to here is whether you will be the *1 in 100* who excels, one of the **52** that hang in there and earn a living, or one of the **47** that in short order exits the business battered and bruised both emotionally and financially. Having to start again from zero—or worse, from less than zero—is not where I want anybody to find themselves.

I can recall one Broker making their industry exit inside the four-year window saying to me, "I can only conclude that people do not like me." This was a person paying not just an economic toll, but clearly an emotional one as well. This person, on paper, had every reason to have been a roaring success yet they could not pull all the pieces together to make it happen.

One area in which their struggle originated was in expending massive amounts of time, energy and dollars on grand plans for nationwide mortgage domination. With less than five transactions under their belt they were lining up meetings with national companies and large unions. At these meetings they were pitching plans, which had they gotten traction would have taken a staff of 50 trained Brokers to deal with.

This lack of focus on the task at hand, on the client at hand, was a critical error.

Success is built one file, one client at a time.

This individual was chasing what they were sure was a massive pot of gold (perpetually) *just* across the horizon. The biggest mistake they made was running so fast towards it, they simply failed to slow down and focus the majority of their time and energy on being the very best Broker they could be for those first few clients. They failed to turn those first few clients into raving fans, or even into a referral of one more file. Their eye was not on the ball; their head was not in the game—they were in a completely different space. A space with no immediate compensation, and thus they could not survive.

This is not an industry, nor is this a book series, about building a multimillion-dollar business with a huge staff. This is largely an industry, and certainly this is a book series, about playing a very important, skilled and rewarding role inside a much larger picture. Yes you will be running your own business, and you will run it like a business, but it is not about scaling up to serve thousands of clients per year. If you find yourself serving 100 clients per year you will have built a remarkable career for yourself, rewarding on all levels.

Attempts to reinvent the wheel in this industry are all too common and completely unnecessary. If Brokers simply mastered all that is currently available to them, they would succeed far beyond their expectations. I am living proof of this.

Who Are You?

DO YOU...
- Thrive on change
- Love challenges
- Enjoy creative thinking
- Enjoy critical thinking
- Like working with numbers
- Crave difficulty
- Desire a dynamic working environment
- Like winning
- Enjoy endurance challenges such as triathlons or iron man competitions
- Search out events that require discipline, focus and consistent training
- Enjoy chatting about meaningful topics
- Have a firm grasp of technology
- Understand the value of written communication

ARE YOU...
- Open minded
- Thoughtful
- Capable of empathy
- Tolerant of rigid policies
- Willing to be told no by clients over and over
- Willing to be told no by lenders over and over
- Willing to show up with a smile every time after all the "no's"

If yes to even half of these, then you are on the right track.

Hustle!

If you instead wish you could turn back the clock 30 years and slow the world down, then Brokering may not be the business for you. The pace of a file is often relentless. Deadlines are a constant pressure.

- The referral source wants you to contact the client now. No, now-now!
- The client wants to discuss their file now.
- The client wants their pre-approval now.
- The client wants to re-confirm their pre-approval now.
- The lender wants the approval documents now.
- The lender wants the appraisal now.
- The client wants the written mortgage commitment now.
- The realtor wants the mortgage approved now.
- The lender wants the signed commitment now.
- The client's lawyer wants the mortgage instructions now.
- The client wants to review the file a week away from completion as their bank has made them a competing offer...now.

Get three to five files on the go at one time, or as we recently had in our office (myself and two assistants) 53 active files, and you very quickly come to realize this is not a part-time job. This is also not a job that you can easily extract yourself from for weeks at a time.

Everything about a client's file is fluid. I've often said, "There are one thousand ways to lose a file." And once we have learned that one thousand we will, I am sure, break new ground on a fresh one thousand.

You make your own success in life. Although you may be handed the work (i.e., the problems to solve), nobody hands you the solutions. The solutions rarely come easy. At first you may not even be handed the work. You will have to go out and find it. Then demonstrate creativity and most of all urgency in handling files for clients. Urgency is the simplest of all things to excel at, and yet it is the one most fail miserably at.

A Broker cannot afford to live in a world of *mañana*. The danger of *tomorrow* is ever present. It lies in wait for you, in the hours you delay submitting your client's file to a lender, or sending the client the mortgage commitment, ordering the appraisal, submitting the client documents to the lender for review—within those hours in which you delay reside many of the one thousand ways to lose a file. You must be ON, on your game, on your email, on your phone.

We strive to...

- Submit all client files to lenders the same day we build them.
- Send complete mortgage commitment/compliance documents packages to clients within an hour of approval from the lender.
- Respond instantly to all incoming calls, emails, texts, etc.

You have to be internally motivated to always be on, to always be delivering a level of service that year after year continues to impress new clients, repeat clients and referral sources alike. Money and/or accolades alone will not be enough to keep that flame burning. You need a deep-seated drive to fuel your motivation. A drive to deliver the goods when it counts, and guess what: it always counts!

A great way to understand your motivation is to understand your personality. And that means taking a personality test, whether it's the Myers-Briggs Type indicator[20], the DISC[21] or any number of other such tests.[22] Sally Hogshead has a new self-assessment tool that is robust and useful as well.[23] It's well worth investing in the one-on-one telephone sessions offered with these tests to gain the perspective of a counsellor who understands the results of your test.[24] Look for your strengths because they are the best basis for growth. Be open to hearing about your weaknesses, acknowledge and accept these weaknesses, but do not obsess over them. There is more to be gained, both in the short and long run by intensifying the focus on further enhancing and fine-tuning your strengths.

I took the DISC personality test a couple of years ago, and it was very enlightening. It indicated that my "natural style" is highly competitive, with a strong ego, and that I am driven by numbers (not dollars per se, just keeping score one way or another). Also that I wish to be influential and persuade others to support my point of view. At my core I cannot deny that this is largely who I am.

---

20 *The Myers & Briggs Foundation*

21 *DISC Personality Testing*

22 *www.16personalities.com* explores another style of measure. With books on each type available from Amazon.

23 *How The World Sees You*: Discover Your Highest Value Through the Science of Fascination – Jun 12 2014 by Sally Hogshead

24 I enjoyed my work with *www.RichScott.ca* of *Focal Point Coaching* re the DISC test.

Know Thyself

The test also measured my "adaptive style." I scored pretty much in the middle, meaning that when required I can tone down my stronger personality traits, I can slow down to socialize and talk about things other than work, like the weather and the kids. I can also throttle back and be analytical when I need to, but this is not my natural tendency.

I've shared the DISC results in several presentations. I've described how when reviewing the report for the first time I came to page 20, which talked about my clients perceptions —specifically how people under moderate to extreme stress might perceive me. It is fair to suggest that most clients of any Mortgage Broker are under moderate to extreme stress. Buying a home, or in many cases buying and selling, along with moving, combined with a sea of foreign paperwork all contribute to a high stress state of mind for any client. And page 20 suggested that people under stress, our clients, might perceive me "as aggressive, overbearing, domineering, hyper -competitive, controlling, etc."

I rolled that around in my head on my way home that evening. When I arrived home, I said to my wife, "Honey, look at page 20 of this report. It basically suggests that I'm an asshole."

My wife, nonplussed, looked squarely at me. "Well, yes, you kind of are."

"What are you talking about?" I said. "I just care about getting things done for my clients. I'm trying to get their file approved as quickly as possible. I'm on a mission to make it happen for them. I want *them* to win."

But that's not necessarily how clients were perceiving my actions or my words.

I turned to my children for support. They were 16 and 18 at the time. "Kids, really? I'm an asshole?"

"You know, Dad, um...sometimes."

And here I thought I was the guy you wanted in your corner. You want to get something done? Give it to me; I'll make it happen. But that's my narrow perception of myself—and not necessarily the perception of somebody sweating out a first-time purchase. Those folks may well perceive me to be something quite different.

So I have embarked on attempts at behaviour change. I am tempering my stronger traits with clients, being less abrupt in emails to my clients, for instance. I understand that efficiency and brevity are easily mistaken for being plain rude.

You will be well served by taking a DISC personality test and confirming where your strengths lie. Brokering is an industry in which having a strong ego makes a difference. Because I can assure you that your ego is going to take a beating. If it is already fragile then this is the sort of industry that will knock it out for the count.

There is a passage in the truly stellar book *The Ultimate Sales*

Machine by Chet Holmes that outlines very succinctly why a high "DI" score, and correspondingly strong ego, work so well for individuals on the front lines with clients.[25] A strong ego evokes emotional resilience. A strong ego inoculates you against the word *no*. The word *no* is simply the response given to a question worded improperly. Pause, re-group, re-phrase and try again.

In business, any "yes" worth getting was preceded by at least one "no."

There is little doubt that the majority of top-producing Brokers, be they mortgage, real estate, insurance or stock Brokers, will all score a high DI. They are not just the go-getters; they are the go-givers.[26] Whatever your assessment, within the strengths you will find evidence of what motivates you, and what motivates you helps direct the path you pursue.

Know your motivation.

Know thyself.

25 *The Ultimate Sales Machine*: Turbocharge Your Business with Relentless Focus on 12 Key Strategies – May 27 2008 by Chet Holmes. *If you read, or listen to, just one more book in your sales career please make it this one.*

26 *The Go-Giver: A Little Story About a Powerful Business Idea – Bob Burg*

CHAPTER 6

THERE ARE NO SHORTCUTS TO SUCCESS

"The pessimist sees difficulty in every opportunity. The optimist sees the opportunity in every difficulty."

— WINSTON CHURCHILL

Each shortcut taken is akin to cutting one of the many strands connecting you to a parachute. You can get away with it for a while, but eventually you cut one too many. The consequences can be dire.

I've already mentioned one of the shortcuts to becoming a licensed Broker. It's paying the $1,000 or so for the "guaranteed pass." I respect the people that create these programs—they are filling a demand in the market. All too many of us want *fast* and *easy*. Show us how to game the system—we will pay extra for that. It's a brilliant business model.

Although perhaps more brilliant still is your paying $20 for this book and discovering that Brokering is hard work, and not "easy money," prior to paying a tutoring premium to get you through a minimally difficult program and into a moderately difficult career, which your temperament may be ill prepared for.

In my estimation, if you're willing to pay for a guaranteed pass, then you're headed for trouble. Once you actually get into this business, you can't buy a guaranteed approval for a client. There is no easy button. You've got to do the work and the work is often difficult and frustrating, and it doesn't always follow a path of logic either. In fact, the lack of logic within the approval process will for many be the toughest thing to adapt to.

Example

I recently worked with a client whose profile was as follows:

- $2.5M-dollar home. Clear title.
- Retired with only CPP and OAS income, no formal pension.
- $1650 per month basement suite rental income.
- $300,000 in stocks and bonds.
- Stellar credit.
- Owner-occupied residence for the past 40 years.
- Accounts with the same bank for 60 years.

This client was referred to me by her bank's branch manager as their current lending guidelines have eliminated "equity" lending and largely discounted rental income. Her own bank could not authorize a $300,000 secured line of credit for her.

No (employment) income = no mortgage. What is required is income that fits the guidelines set out by the federal government, or more specifically each lender's unique interpretation of the federal government guidelines.

No doubt this sounds like it lacks logic. Clearly, this client has significant security to pledge, and more than enough real-world income with which to service the $300-per-month minimum payment due.

This is reflective of the trends in the current lending landscape in Canada.

One could argue that the (current) licensing program doesn't equip you to succeed as a Broker. And as things stand this would be a fair argument. But what the course does do is act as a sort of litmus test for your brain. Are you capable of learning, retaining and regurgitating 65% of this data? If not, if you can't absorb it on your own without help, then you're in trouble. This business is unforgiving of people who take shortcuts and find themselves in need of help.

Another form of a shortcut is continuing to work part time. This shortcut can quickly cost you your reputation and your clients. I've heard Brokers say, "I'm going to keep working 40 hours a week at the plant/mill/shop/office and will just Broker mortgages on weekends and evenings."

No, you won't.

A part-time performer is not a top performer. A part-time performer is a non-performer. In this industry, part-timers don't succeed. They certainly do not offer their clients the very best possible knowledge, service or experience.

Walk a Mile in Your Client's Shoes

Recall your own financing experience with your first home, like phoning the various parties involved at all hours of the day and night for answers to various questions or to talk through various points of concern. And if you couldn't reach your banker or Broker between 9am and 5pm, you were especially unhappy. Calling in a panic over some piece of the puzzle at 1:01pm and not getting a call back until 5:01pm—well no doubt you would not tolerate that long before shopping for a new Broker yourself.

Brokers cannot afford to put more than an hour, let alone four hours, of silence between themselves and clients during the workday. This is an unacceptable concept. Unacceptable to the clients, the Realtors, the lenders, the referral sources, to the market as a whole. Slow responses are hardly acceptable during evenings and over weekends, let alone during regular office hours. Clients expect prompt responses or they'll fire their Brokers.

In addition, the reality is that the best way to learn this business is by doing. Only by doing can your application intake and underwriting skills improve. You've got to get in the game and work files regularly, as many as you can. Hone your skills. Take any and every application you can in the early days, just for the practice alone.

As long as you're hanging onto the regular and steady pay-cheque from an unrelated (unfocused) or even semi-related (semi-focused) job, you're unlikely to find significant success as a Broker. The reasons are twofold. First, your primary focus and attention won't be on Brokering mortgages. Second, you have a safety net. The longer you cling to that safety net the more rigid your fingers become. Taking the leap is scary, but you're more likely to succeed with a clear and unimpeded focus on one thing: to be the better Broker.

It's a Mortgage Emergency

It has been said there's no such thing as a *mortgage emergency*. We Brokers may know that no underwriter is going to be reviewing documents late at night or over the weekend. However, we also know from experience that responding to those late phone calls, or emails over the weekend, often goes miles towards calming a stressed client. If you can be the one to put them at ease promptly whenever they need it, you will establish a solid relationship and reputation. For the clients, their concern constitutes a mortgage emergency.

As your business matures, and your skills evolve, you may consider things like a professional answering service, knowing that indeed there are no mortgage emergencies that truly need your attention until the following weekday morning. But you are a few years away from this level.

In the early years, if a client calls at 9:37pm on Friday night while you're having dinner with friends and you let the call go to voicemail, watch out. When clients call, especially early in a file, you better be available 24/7. Otherwise, there are always Brokers hungrier than you who will be available 24/7. When Brokers don't answer the phone, they risk their clients talking about their concerns with friends and relatives, who may pose even more questions, thus elevating the client's concerns that much more. Then that relative says, "Let's try my Broker. They always answer their phone."

Now you've given another Broker the opportunity to help your client. They may provide answers that relieve your client's stress or they may reply in such a way that raises doubts about your skills handling the file. So please understand that for the first one or two years, you've got to be a 24/7 Broker. The need for this can be mitigated once you are better established.

Always On

I like to tell the story of a Realtor who earned his success by passing out his business card saying, "Guaranteed call-back in one hour." That's an important hook because the average response time by real estate agents is way longer than an hour. So that's how this guy broke into the business, responding quickly 24/7. Over the next year as his client list grew and active clients consumed more of his time, he could no longer respond to calls within an hour. Nor did he need to.

He changed his business card to read, "Guaranteed call-back within 24 hours." As he added more clients over the following year, he dropped all references to call-backs completely. His card now simply lists his name and number. That's one way to start a business: rapidly adding new clients who provide referrals for potential new clients. The circle grows bigger and bigger because the Broker is available 24/7 for the first couple of years.

To be clear, 24/7 has in my experience elicited few calls earlier than 8am or later than 8pm. The rare calls outside those hours tend to be brief, with many callers having expected to get voicemail, yet quite happy to have an instant answer.

Brokers, like bankers, typically work Monday through Friday, although the workday can stretch well into the evening. My weekends are usually very quiet. I don't often hear from clients unless I text, email or call them first, or unless they are experiencing one of those rare mortgage emergencies.

Clients tend to be working with their Realtors over the weekends, and once the offer is accepted they prefer to relax on the weekends and holidays leading up to their completion date.

During the workweek, my lunch hour has practically disappeared. This is prime time for clients, especially couples, to set appointments or conference calls with their Broker. It makes sense for clients to call at midday and in the evenings after work because that's when they're free. So Brokers often need to be available during those times, typically 8am until 8pm.

There are no real shortcuts around the hours of availability you need to provide; there is flexibility though. Squeezing in various mid-day events is far more manageable as you are the director of your own workdays, which can be as much of a curse as a blessing.

It's Not Personal, It's Just Business!

In the early days of your career, any long-standing friendships you may have with top-producing Realtors rarely translate into new clients for you. This can cause a rift in the friendship when the hard realities are not addressed up front.

Such individuals may prove to be excellent resources, providing insight and support, or even mentoring you as you enter the business. Successful (*ergo*, busy) people are often generous with their time and expertise. Cultivating these relationships can have longstanding material benefits to your business...just not in the manner you expected. A mentor is valuable in a different way than a referral source, but still valuable.

My point here—and it may be hard to understand at first—is don't expect these industry connections, even the lifelong best buddies, to refer all (or any) of their business to you. It will almost certainly not happen. And they will not want to tell you this up front. Why would they? Think about it: if they lay out the hard truth up front they risk losing a friend. If they say nothing at all, well hey, maybe you don't actually enroll. Maybe you don't pass the exam, maybe you don't follow through. So it is better they say nothing until the last possible minute. This is a reasonable thing when you think about it, although it will seem less reasonable when it is a reality.

Why do I suggest they are unlikely to hand you a stack of business on a silver platter?

Aside from the simple fact that the friendship is again put at great risk when a transaction goes wrong, there is a bigger issue. Rookies need to understand that people performing at the top of their game like to work with others in the same league. Top-producing Realtors often have long-term relationships that are near unbreakable with established Brokers, in many instances having worked together through stressful transactions that in turn strengthened those relationships. So they are unlikely to make room for you on the basis of friendship alone. On the basis of excellence is another story.

A Realtor's commission is typically 3% to 5% of the purchase price. Few Realtors are willing to put that commission—and more important, that client relationship—in the hands of a brand-new inexperienced Broker. They will stick with the Broker with whom they've completed the last 50 files. Realtors, like anybody, want stability and predictability. They do not want to put their commission on the line, and beyond that, they do not want to put their relationship with the client on the line by referring them to a greenhorn.

I do suggest that new Brokers cultivate relationships with top people in the field. Just don't throw any guilt their way for not sending business your way. In fact, you want to acknowledge that you understand precisely why they're not able to refer clients to you...yet. Over the years as you stay in their orbit you will gain their trust, confidence and eventually their business. But first just be looking for their wisdom—this is a huge icebreaker. Appeal to their sense of mastery; ask for a brief monthly meeting or even just a brief monthly call to talk about the business of business. That will keep you on their radar as you slowly increase your own skill level and experience.

Then, should their current Broker drop the ball, you will be there to pick it up and run confidently with it.

Asking somebody to put their livelihood in your hands is a big ask. A referral is a transfer of trust. So you've got to be respectful and you've got to understand that until you build the trust, until you build a book of business of your own and earn a solid reputation, you may not wind up with all of the business you think you're going to get from that old friend.

If you doubt any of this, just try calling them out directly on the points made here and see what their response is. You must do this in person though, as you want an accurate face-to-face read.

Be humble and be understanding, whatever reaction may come.

Calm, Cool, and Collected

How you portray yourself to others, especially in the face of challenging news, is critical to your success. If you are warm, generous and smiling, people around you are likely to be the same. If you're a black cloud, you'll probably attract other people filled with gloom and doom. Or you may find yourself alone. Alone is obviously not a path to success.

Be proactive, as I have outlined above. Do not be reactive. Absorb news, digest it, and then act calmly with logic and forethought.

A short-fused reactor is not someone any of us wants to be around.

You need to be optimistic and believe you've got the stuff to succeed. If you believe in yourself, others will believe in you. Confidence is contagious. If you're a believer, they'll become a believer. A lot of people are like Jekyll and Hyde. Out in the world they're happy-go-lucky, but behind closed doors with their buddy—perhaps that top-producing Realtor buddy— they're cranky or embittered or prejudiced. People can see through facades and they're not likely to provide referrals to those who wear two faces. It is also human nature to avoid frank discussions of these realities with each other. Pay attention to the types of people you open up with, and the ones that you shut down with. Then act accordingly.

Again, forming this sort of thoughtful calm approach is not simple; it is not instant. This is Brokering. Learning to work with the longer, slower flow of communication in all aspects of life will prove fruitful in your career.

Each day too many of us choose not to speak frankly on a wide array of topics, because to do so only creates challenges. Often needless challenges. So we all go along to get along to some extent. However, when it comes to choosing a career path, you must seek out those who will speak the truth to you. Even if it is a hard truth.

Are you pursuing shortcuts? In some cases I hope you are (like listening to audiobooks at double speed), but be aware that any shortcuts you are counting on to launch your business may in fact turn into dead ends once the rubber hits the road. Re-evaluate all the things you think will make your start in Brokering "easy" or "quick" and work on the counterargument just to be aware of the potential challenges that may in fact exist.

Always count on having to take the long, and lonely, way there.

CHAPTER 7

QUESTION EVERYTHING AND EVERYONE

"Your mind is like water, when agitated it becomes difficult to see but if allowed to settle, the answer becomes clear."

— TSEM TULKU RINPOCHE

During my first few months as a licensed Broker, I called on ten top producers in our company. Each made time for me, which in itself made a lasting and influential impression on me. It was interesting how far ranging each of their personal styles was. In some meetings, we hardly spoke about the business. Instead, we spoke of personal philosophies, the world around us, and life in general. Others were all business, methodical and analytical. They drilled down into the nitty-gritty details of underwriting a client's file. In hindsight, I should have recorded every meeting and compiled pages of notes. Nonetheless, those meetings helped shape my approach, and much of the content remains the foundation of how I approach the business today. My approach? Methodical, thoughtful and with unflinching optimism. There is always a solution to be found.

One key takeaway from these meetings, which I have in turn shared with newer Brokers many times over "position yourself as an expert" has had a profound effect on my approach to life and to business. After all, the only way one can hope to become an expert is by first studying, then doing.[27] And so I approach both the studying and the doing with a beginner's mind each day.[28] In an ongoing effort to position myself as an expert. With awareness that "expert" is a path, not a destination.

Other lessons included always speaking with confidence, sounding strong and alert. Specifically over the telephone as the ability to make a good first impression is limited to tone and inflection. Have no doubt that your physical posture and mental state come through the other end of the phone line clearly. Be upright; be awake. One Broker informed me that tonality is three times more influential than the actual content. At the time I did not even think to question this three-to-one statistic, for it was delivered with such booming confidence that the point was made indelibly.

---

27 Studying—there is no "School" of Brokering in which to enroll, and studying another Broker day-to-day is not an advisable way to learn the business. Studying comes down to consuming as many books on human behaviour and on business as possible. It's paying attention and noting each lesson learned from each client interaction and working every single application offered.

28 I first heard the phrase "beginner's mind" in "*Buddhism For Busy People*: Finding Happiness In An Uncertain World" May 15 2008 by David Michie. Mr. Michie has written several useful books on mixing meditation and the tenets of Buddhism into modern life.

What you say matters, i.e., having the technical proficiency.

How you say it matters more, i.e., sounding like you are alert and confident in what you are saying.

Share Your Best Ideas

What sank in the deepest from these meetings was how all of these top performers had in common the willingness to make time for a rookie in the business. I paid attention to that lesson. A few years later when I spoke to a group of over 300 Mortgage Brokers in my hometown, I said, "My office is right off the #1 highway, a couple of exits down from this venue. My door is always open. If anybody wants to talk about the business of business, I'd be happy to do so."

Over the following 12 months, only three of those 300+ Brokers accepted my offer. I make no claims to being the mortgage oracle, but my business seems to be doing what many other Brokers want their businesses to be doing. Why not take 30 minutes and stop in? I suspect the percentage that did probably correlates to the number of Brokers entering the business that will build a successful long-term career: one in 100.

It is also a perfect example of why you can be generous with your ideas. I have given away more ideas than I will ever be able to act upon, and I have been given amazing ideas from others that would change my business; but finding the time and energy to implement them is the challenge that each of us faces.

The beauty of idea (information) exchange is that it is exponential.

When you exchange goods with someone, the number of goods does not change. You each value what the other has to offer and so the exchange is a "win-win." But think about the exchange of ideas. If you have an idea, and I have an idea, and we share our ideas, now we each walk away with two ideas apiece. But even more interesting is how ideas can mingle with each other and multiply and spin off hybrid ideas. You might walk away with five new ideas once you factor in the information that I have shared. Keeping ideas to yourself is the worst idea of all. Share. Ask others what they know, and in return offer them what you know.

Unlimited Questions

As a Broker, you must offer clients samples of the knowledge you possess in order to draw from them vital pieces of data that they may not think important enough to share with you.

Clients are thinking A to B. "So, what's your best rate?"

Brokers need to be thinking A to Z.

A. Variable or Fixed?

B. If fixed, 1 yr., 2yr., 3 yr., 4yr, 5 yr., (Never 7 yr. nor 10 yr.)?[29]

C. If variable, which lender? Features vary greatly between lenders.

D. With a line of credit feature or without?

E. 20% down or less, can they reach 20% down?

F. Portability from one province to the next?

G. Specific plans around lump-sum penalties.

H. Any as-yet-unnamed parties that will need to be on title?

I. Any parties on the application that prefer not to be on title?

J. Will title be held in the name of a holding company?

K. Origins of down payment?

L. Are all applicants' income taxes filed and up-to -date?

M. Is there a commission, bonus or overtime component to the income?

---

29 The prepayment penalties that accompany longer-term fixed-rate products combined with market conditions from the mid-80's and the increasingly shorter period that clients remain in their mortgage terms have conspired to keep me from writing a single mortgage beyond a five-year term, despite the lure of up to double the commission to do so. Solutions for the client are paramount, NOT solutions for the Broker!

N. If part time, are the hours guaranteed?

O. Is the client's current banking done with an institution we have access to?

P. Are there debts not showing on one credit report that might show on the other?

Q. Does the client own any other real estate?

R. Was their previous mortgage insured (i.e., CMHC)?

S. If yes, does it make mathematical sense to pay the top-up premium?

T. Is the client aware of all of the other related taxes and legal fees?

U. If a new build, were builder incentives in the contract?

V. Was the property ever a grow-op or drug lab?

W. Are extensive upgrades planned?

X. Are they considering knocking the home down and rebuilding?

Y. Is this a fix and flip, or a long-term hold?

Z. Oh yeah...so what's the best rate factoring in the answers above?

There is another set or two of A–Z questions to ask throughout an application and transaction. The questions above and the ones unlisted will be addressed in depth in Volume 2, once you are licensed and starting to speak the language of the business.

The point is that you, the Broker, have the ability to save your clients thousands, sometimes tens of thousands, of dollars. You've also got the power to lose them the same amount of money. Recognizing this and understanding your influence over clients and their files can be overwhelming when you realize how little you know. Clients view you as the professional (mind reader) in the equation. They put more faith in their Broker than they should, and clients always ask too few questions. It is on the Broker to ask questions. If you're new to the business, you may not deserve the client's faith, but you will (likely) be granted it and must respect it. Never be afraid to ask your clients, your fellow Brokers, your lenders a seemingly stupid question. In this business, stupid questions save files. Stupid questions save clients (from themselves). Stupid questions save Brokers from losing clients, referral sources or worse.

Remind your clients often that there are no stupid questions and that they should ask you every single little thing that pops into their heads. This can be pivotal.

Always be asking questions yourself, of your office manager, your managing Broker, lenders' representatives and underwriters. Quiz the Realtor, the appraiser and the real estate lawyer. Always, always ask questions. If it flashes across your mind, write it down or email it to somebody. Ask that question and get an answer.

I prefer to risk being viewed as stupid by somebody rather than to be sued by them. The questions asked through a file may seem silly, but on occasion can make all the difference.

Clients and Brokers alike lose when questions go unasked and thus unanswered. Problems arise at complex points, which could have been averted earlier on in the process. As an example, six out of ten Canadian homeowners will break their fixed-rate mortgage at an average of 38 months. In other words, they break their existing mortgage agreement early and in almost every case incur pre-payment penalties. Most homeowners had no idea of the nature and size of penalty coming their way because bankers and Brokers historically were not trained to explain them in detail up front. I lay out examples with clear dollar amounts to new clients in the first ten minutes of our initial phone conversation. I will share the scripts in Volume 2, as they have become a vital step in positioning me in the new client's mind as an expert, as an educator, thereby differentiating my services from those of the last person they spoke with.

Script Sample:

All too often mortgage penalties come in the form of an "interest-rate differential." This land mine is buried in the majority of five-year fixed-rate mortgages. The penalty is often the equivalent of ~4% of the mortgage balance. In contrast, variable-rate mortgages (often perceived as "the risky choice") carry a prepayment penalty of just

~0.5%. In reality, the five-year fixed mortgage is arguably far riskier because the financial penalty for breaking that mortgage is variable and is ~eight times greater than that of a variable rate mortgage.

People break mortgages for many reasons. The answer as to how and why requires a short walk through the lives of two young single people.

A single man from one side of town buys a studio apartment and signs a five-year fixed mortgage because his parents tell him this is the safe product. Meanwhile, a single woman from the other side of town buys a studio in the same building, and takes the same advice from her parents. They really like this building for their daughter because it has rental restrictions, something parents seem to love. Inevitably, our two buyers meet, and over a three-year period they fall in love and move in together. Suddenly finding themselves with one too many studio apartments, and no ability to retain and rent one, they must sell the first. At this point they trigger their first IRD (interest-rate differential) penalty. They learn the hard way about the illogical formula used.

Then less than a year later as the couple find themselves moving from their current province to another to pursue an employment opportunity, they learn the hard lesson that a Credit Union mortgage cannot be transferred from one province to another. As such, they pay their second mortgage penalty.

In neither case were they able to retain the property as a rental, which would have been more appealing than triggering a penalty ~4% of the mortgage balance and paying Realtors' fees.

This story of course carries on, but I try to keep it short and focus on the happy reasons that clients break mortgages. Between you and me, the next chapter of the story may go like this:

They then buy a larger home for their growing family in the new province and once again they lock in that "safe" five-year fixed mortgage, at least avoiding credit unions this time around. But they stick with a chartered bank because they want to be with a national lender just in case they get transferred somewhere else. Then there's another change in their lives, one that affects 60% of marriages within ten years: divorce. And with neither party able to qualify for the current mortgage balance on their own they are forced to sell the property and break the mortgage, again triggering an IRD.

Each party will subsequently buy another property, usually a smaller one, which overlooks the fact that we humans like to pair bond and before long our applicants will be on the move once again.

You get the idea. As a Broker, if you're not explaining prepayment penalties to clients on day one, then the clients may pay dearly for your oversight. First-time buyers aren't remotely thinking about breaking their mortgage because they don't even have a mortgage yet. So it seems almost counterintuitive. Yet, as I point out to clients, they are looking at A to B, and I am looking at A to Z for their benefit. Neither of us wants to be having a truly painful conversation 38 months from now.

So, ask questions!

Get the clients thinking and speaking. Do your job thoroughly.

Do not be an order taker. Order takers are lazy; order takers make lame statements when things go wrong like, "They never told me X," or, "Well I just gave the client what they asked for."

Be an expert advisor. The #1 component of advising is asking questions. The expert does not give a client what a client asks for; rather, the expert asks a client why they want that product. Once they get the first answer they ask why one more time, maybe two or three more times, digging deeper for the details.

Order takers do not receive referrals; instead, they risk being reviled by their clients.

Be referred or be reviled. It is your choice.

CHAPTER 8

SUIT UP AND SHOW UP!

"You will never get a second chance to make a first impression."
— WILL ROGERS

99% of women grasp this concept, and I am not about to offer any high-end fashion advice here; however, 99% of men will need to pay close attention to this. All too many men find as many excuses as possible to dress down.

The fact is you would be hard pressed to arrive at any event and be considered irreparably overdressed. De-tuning is easy. Lose the tie, undo a button or two, and roll up your sleeves. However, showing up underdressed is common for men and next to impossible to correct on the spot.

Appearances matter. At the very least you need to go into the world each day well groomed and dressed in professional attire. Yes, our parents taught us that it's what's on the inside that counts, and while that may be true the fact remains that clean, fresh-pressed and colour-coordinated wrapping makes a tremendous difference in our perceptions of what a person is about.

You cannot get around basic human nature. You can lament it, but you cannot change it.

You're dealing with clients' largest asset(s), specifically the largest single debt(s) attached to that most important asset. Showing up in a hoodie and sweats will not inspire confidence.

I've known new Brokers who finance fancy cars to create an image. I say to them, "Dude, nice car! Too bad half of your clients live in apartment buildings and will never see it. The other half you will deal with by phone." Maybe one in 50 clients is going to see this car, and maybe 1 in 100 of them will think a thought about it. They tell me driving in style makes them feel good. I ask, why take on the debt and burn up capital you could invest in your business? But certainly, buying a decent suit makes sense. Within reason!

Here's a true story: There is a local Broker who has now lost two sets of clients to me, and likely several others, partly because they choose Starbucks as their office, which is their first mistake, and then arrive looking ready for a Zumba class, the second and often fatal error. Yes we are all about fitness and being active here in Vancouver, but there is a time for Lululemons and that time is not business meeting time.

When those same clients later met with me, and found me

wearing a suit and tie, located in a professional space within a lawyer's head office, the Zumba Broker never had a chance.

This is a serious profession; treat it as such. Your clients expect you to.

You'll want to invest a few dollars in some professional-looking clothes if you don't already dress professionally. If you need convincing, take a look at the video shot in Austin Texas of the difference in revenues generated by a homeless gentleman once he suited up.[30] If a stranger is more likely to give you money on the street when you're dressed in a suit, rather than in casual attire, what does that say about the odds of them giving you their mortgage business?

That's the way it works in business and in life. A professional appearance inspires confidence, and a professional demeanor inspires trust.

The reverse is not the case though. You will be judged, but you best not do any judging of your own.

A Brush With Fame

In 1992, I was in a nightclub one Saturday night and ran into a friend from high school. Last I had heard, said friend had taken off to Los Angeles to make it happen as a script supervisor in the movie business (she subsequently did amazingly well). Christina turned to the fellow she was there with and

---

30 *https://www.youtube.com/watch?v=w1rwRT229Uo* "The Real Homeless Man Experiment." It says it all, in a rather sad way.

introduced him to my girlfriend and I. "Ethan," he said, "Nice to meet you." I scanned his ill-fitting pizza-stained t-shirt draped across a budding premature paunch on his otherwise athletic frame and thought to myself, *Wow, this guy is maybe 21 and he has already given up.* The conversation was brief.

The following year sitting in a theatre reading *Premiere* magazine, I caught the profile on the star of the movie we were about to watch; I was struck by his dedication to the role and how in the months leading up to shooting the film he packed away ice cream and pizza nonstop to gain an extra 30 pounds, which he would shed during filming for added realism. The film was "Alive," released in 1993, starring Ethan Hawke.[31]

This was a painful example of meeting a man, passing immediate judgment based on his appearance, and neglecting to have what might have been an insightful conversation. After all, didn't we all meet the most important people in our lives by having a conversation? Turning and walking away from someone is turning and walking away from opportunity. You can never know what opportunity you are in fact walking away from...not by a stained T-shirt you can't, anyway.

That experience has stuck with me—it was good to learn that lesson early on in life.

You can't fix under-dressed and you can't fix the snap judgments others will make of you. You can fix your wardrobe,

---

31 "Alive" (1993): A fact-based chronicle of a Uruguayan rugby team's struggle to survive after their plane crashes in the Andes.

and more important, you can fix your own snap-judgments of others.

However, the fact remains that most of us are going to give some extra time and attention to a professionally dressed person over one in jeans and a golf shirt. Your clients will too.

It is good to be a guy on shopping days.

For men, looking professional is simple. Add two or three suits and a few white dress shirts to your wardrobe and you are set. When I started, I went to the factory outlet stores and bought three $99 designer label suits. I spent another $60 each with a professional tailor and seven years later still collect the odd compliment on one of them. Two of them I recently retired, which I was OK with.

1.5 wears per week

78 wears per year

468 wears over 6 years

$159 cost

34 cents per wear

I'm not qualified to address professional dress for women. And I don't need to; women already know more about appearance than I ever will. No doubt many were rolling their eyes at my thirty-four-cent math.

Change It Up

Before I became a Broker, I ran a high-performance automotive parts business. My clients were 16 to 25-year-old males worried more about how their car looked than how the guy behind the counter looked. I typically wore t-shirts and jeans that wound up greasy by the end of the day. I didn't worry about polishing my footwear. I wore steel-toed work boots to protect my toes while taking the forklift for a spin. I shaved every second or third day.

When I became a Broker, adjusting people's perceptions of me without breaking the bank was important. As I have said, you can arrive at a beach party in a three-piece suit and make it work. You can always remove a jacket and tie if you don't need them, but you can't just conjure them up from thin air if you do need them.

So suit up and show up.

Early on, I attended almost every real estate-related or finance-related event I could find in our city. I showed up ready to walk the walk, clean-shaven and wearing one of my $99 suits, with a pocketful of classy business cards.

I joined the Chamber of Commerce (which lasted just one year), The Real Estate Action Group (seven years and counting) and The Real Estate Investment Network (which lasted three years), and subscribed to key local business publications, *BC Business* magazine and the *Business in Vancouver* newspaper, both of which I still review thoroughly. The magazine and newspaper continue to be excellent sources for local business events, although admittedly I attend far fewer at this point as my time is better spent being attentive to the database I have grown than adding further clients to it.

Carpe Momentum!

At each of these events, if I ran into somebody I knew and hadn't seen in a while, or struck up an interesting conversation with someone new, I would make a point of connecting with that person again soon after. All too often we run into people, have a quick chat and in parting say to one another, "We should get together sometime for a coffee or lunch." And that is where it ends.

Instead seize these comments and actualize them. "In fact, I am back downtown again Monday and Tuesday of next week for mid-morning meetings; I could make either a coffee or a lunch work on either day."

95% of the time we would schedule something right then and there, as opposed to never at all, as is so often the case.

The odds were that I in fact had no plans to be back downtown the following week, but I wanted to make it easy to find a yes; I wanted to create four potential times to meet in a low-pressure sort of way.

Now that I did in fact have an appointment, I would in turn try to leverage off that meeting at least one or two more in the area.

From these additional meetings there would inevitably be

additional opportunities to either meet or be introduced to others. Of all the many books I have read, books on networking were not on the list. Perhaps reading a few on power networking might have honed my skills further, but I always loathed the concept of "networking." It conjures in my mind dystopian images of robotic interaction for no purpose other than perpetuating the self. Networking to network. The end result a hollow shell of frail and baseless "connections." These events seem like an archaic, slow motion and much frailer form of LinkedIn.

All of the meetings I had were with people I genuinely liked; life is too short to meet with and to work with people you do not like.

I still suit up every day, but now I mostly show up at the office only. I do miss the three to four coffee meetings and lunches per week, and the occasional dinner meeting as well. However, my business has evolved beyond having the time for such meetings, and you would be correct in wondering how long I can be significantly less social and remain as busy as I am currently. I wonder as well.

So gents, spend an extra few dollars on a shirt with buttons that go all the way down the front, get that off-the-rack suit tailored, polish those shoes weekly. It only costs a little extra to go first class.

Then get your shiny self out there and interact with the world; out there in the world is where the magic happens at first.

Once you start bringing the magic in the door we can talk about casual Fridays, but not before.

CHAPTER 9

MANAGE YOUR BEHAVIOUR, AND YOUR TIME TAKES CARE OF ITSELF

"Only put off until tomorrow what you are willing to die having left undone."

— PABLO PICASSO

Why waste the effort you just put into suiting up? Maximize it.

When leaving my office for a business meeting, I always have more than one place to go. I schedule coffee, lunch or dinner around events. You impress upon people your commitment to your craft when you tell them you're headed to or from a corporate event. It makes clear that you are on a mission to learn and to improve yourself. And if the meeting is after the event, you can talk about what you learned.

Mission Creep

In Brokering, as in life, time is the most precious resource. Today, more than ever, time is an easy thing to have slip through your fingers, one post, like, tweet and pin at a time. "Time management" is an outdated term. Today the focus needs to be on behaviour management.

Your behaviour is the root of how you spend your time, and thus dictates how much time you have available for various tasks.

When you are beholden to nobody but yourself, as is the case with Brokering, you're vulnerable to "mission creep." That's a term the military uses to describe a situation where the scope of an original mission expands far beyond the original objective. Often one success leads to a slightly greater risk taken, and so on, until a catastrophic failure occurs.

We suffer from Facebook-creep when we intend to spend a few seconds posting a quick pic or one-liner and instead wind up spending an hour surfing our feed and checking back for "success" via likes and shares of our posts. Google-creep occurs when we intend to search for details on a listing down the block, which expands to homes within a 5-kilometre radius, and then a quick download of a Szechuan chicken recipe for dinner tonight, which contains a link to the latest celebrity fiasco, which triggers a quick search on YouTube for that video said celebrity made in the 80s, and a quick peek at the weather forecast, or whatever. Poof, another hour passes. What happened to your original search? Can you even recall what you started out looking for? Mission creep.

For a number of years, I kept a sticky note with the word "Focus" on top of my computer monitor. I removed myself from the email lists of various jokers and ranters, stopped logging in to YouTube or Facebook during office hours and started tracking the number of hours spent at my desk. The goal was to spend less time there. A 30-minute session on Facebook mid-day only makes me 30 minutes later to return home. For some it means 30 minutes less work done, but a Broker has specific tasks that are deadline dependent and so must be done before leaving the office.

Many people believe they "work" 60 hours a week, though their browser history and mobile phone records would likely indicate otherwise. While perhaps planted in their office for 12 hours per day, many of those hours cannot be counted as productive. Consider implementing some levels of self-regulation, such as a work-only phone number and ignoring your personal cell phone during the workday. I acknowledge that I cannot be without a phone, and I acknowledge that as long as my work phone is in my hand I will respond to work-related calls, texts and emails at all hours. Know thyself.

Tech Tips

Move to a cloud-based secure solution for email. Do it this week, or today. Pick one that allows storage and access to all of your data and documents across all of your devices. You should be able to add a new contact card, send or delete an email from your phone, tablet, laptop or desktop and have your mailboxes and devices instantly sync with each other.

Look at Google's solution: consider Microsoft365. Go with what you are used to. Learning a new computer system while learning a new trade is unnecessarily complicating.

Due to the nature of the data I work with, I do not have laptop computers—which are rapidly becoming dated devices—and no data is stored on any one device. I could lose my phone tomorrow, and within minutes have the data remotely wiped from the password-protected device, then buy a new one within the hour and have all of the exact data restored. Seamless.

A desktop PC need only serve very basic office purposes; they do not need to be amazing high-speed machines. Even the slowest of desktops today is amazingly fast for all Brokering-related tasks. But one behaviour that is an absolute must is being paperless. To effectively do this requires dual monitors. Have the exact same machine and keyboard at your proper office as you do your home office. Set up the browsers and any folders identically. This will allow seamless transition from one office to the other. The dual monitors will allow you to open documents on one screen and transfer that data into the mortgage application software on the other screen, all without having to hit print, reload toner (or worse, go pick up toner), find a fresh stack of paper, walk to the printer, input the data and then shred the documents afterward. This will save you thousands of hours over your career.

Keep it simple, spend a few extra dollars and be paperless from day one.

Do Not Try To Be the Expert of All Things

Always defer to experts in their field. Not the sales guys at the big-box electronics store; rather a dedicated IT professional who is available to help pick out, set up and maintain the correct machine and software. Spend a few extra dollars on quality advice and support. Trying to read up on computers and sorting out which is the correct one on your own is akin to your client trying to work through the products and policies of 30 different lenders; it is time lost that could be spent focusing on more important, useful and relevant data or skills.

A few courses on how to use Microsoft Office may be time well spent. Application shortcuts are vital to know. Basic skills are all that is required; make sure you have them prior to starting this new career.

The next few paragraphs may seem like a shift from the topic of time management, but I assure you they are not. Stick with me here.

New = Different = Scary

We humans have a tendency to stick with the familiar. Buried in some ancient part of our brains is a fear of the different. "It seems different...danger...kill it," has largely given way to, "It seems different...danger...ignore it." The most significant area where this mindset can cause problems is with the most powerful time management tool ever invented. Sorry, but credit goes not to Doc Brown from "Back to the Future," but to Alexander Graham Bell.

The telephone triggers a flight response in many of us. We do not want to call strangers, and interestingly we often do not like to answer incoming calls from strangers. One exception is people who see an unfamiliar number on their screen as a reason to call back and challenge the caller on their intent, as if somehow slighted by the digital intrusion—yet willing to inconvenience themselves further by calling back. We humans can be conflicted and complicated beings. 'Call reluctance' is real, and to be avoided or overcome.

Perhaps for my generation the terror triggered at the sound of a ringing phone was deeply implanted with the 1979 thriller "When a Stranger Calls," the next generation less so when the 2006 remake came out.

Whatever the reason, many of us do not like calling people we don't know, and tend to let calls from new or 'unknown' numbers go to voicemail. So let's focus positively on **forming two new habits**.

1. Answer incoming calls immediately

Do not let it go to voicemail. We hesitate to answer because of fear of "the unknown, the different." That little almond-size piece of our brain called the amygdala, our flight-or-fight response mechanism, has far too much control over our daily habits. It comes up with a thousand reasons why you shouldn't change anything in your life. It's what is left of the cave person's brain in your head today trying to protect you from dangers that no longer exist.

A brightly coloured ringing phone is not a danger, yet we pause: *amygdala.*

The stranger approaching us at the business mixer, where (remind yourself) we came to meet strangers, gives us pause: *amygdala.*

When you see a stick on the ground, you avoid it unconsciously because your brain instantly processes the possibility that it might be a snake: *amygdala.*[32] (OK, this reaction might be worth hanging onto.)

Retrain your brain, learn to answer that phone on the first ring, no matter who the caller is. Also, those "unknown number" calls, they tend to be from members of law enforcement or other government agencies—wonderful applicants. Either that or you have won a free cruise. Regardless, start answering every single phone call—politely—from now on. Start building this crucial habit.

How does this relate to time management? The time you waste letting that call go to voicemail, never mind the rapidly decreasing chances that the caller will leave a voicemail at all, and then the time spent listening to the message that hopefully offers a name and a number with a request for a call-back, that time is gone forever. Multiple minutes wasted

32 *Risk: The Science and Politics of Fear* by Dan Gardner. An excellent book on the topic of irrational fears.

so you could stay in your comfort zone. Meanwhile, by the time you call back you get their voicemail and now you are playing tag. Except you get no second call. Why, you ask? Because the referring Realtor gave the client the contact data for three different Brokers and the potential client is now on the phone with the next one, because that Broker picked up. Always pick up.

Move out of the comfort zone and into the top-producer zone.

2. Always call back instantly

What about when you cannot pick up? This next tip depends upon your living entirely through a single cell-phone number, which is precisely what you should be doing in the early years. You can have pre-set text responses, which allow you to communicate to the new caller that you will be calling them back once finished with your current call. I have a few different pre-set messages.

"Thank you for calling. I am with clients at the moment but will return your call as soon as I can."

"Thank you for calling. I am currently on another call and will be back to you as soon as possible."

"Thank you for calling. I am attending a presentation for the next hour or so. Please text or email if urgent, otherwise I will call back during the next break."

- You will immediately call a referral when the contact data is sent to you. It is your number-one priority. When somebody asks you to call, you will call. *Instantly*. Build this habit on a personal level—it is part of the new you.

On a professional level many clients have been more than a little impressed when I have called within minutes of my referral source sending me the new client's contact data. The best scenario is you reach the new clients before their meeting with the referral source has even ended. Not only are you impressing the client with your response time, you are impressing the referral source too. And what is a referral? It is a transfer of trust. What else is it? It is an opportunity for you to make that referral source look good, to look like they know action-oriented people (you).

Next to the telephone, and its effective use, the second-best time management tool is an actual office-office. Being away from home is a choice I make to further focus my time. When I am in my office it is not to socialize, to surf the net aimlessly or to sit back and read. It is to lean forward and work clients' files. All of my writing is done from my home office, as are big-picture tasks. But from Monday to Friday I am in the client zone, which is my professional office space.

Fear is internal

Leaping into a new career induces a number of fears, even though you're more likely to slip and fall in your bathtub than you are to botch a career change. Embrace optimism. You are already on the right track as you are taking the time to read an entire book about your prospective new career. For the optimists out there, the opportunities have never been greater.[33] Technology is creating new opportunities every day.

Our biggest threat to future success is ourselves. What's the top reason people don't sign up for the Mortgage Broker course? They say they don't have time. Let's think about that. If you work a 40-hour week plus a few hours of overtime and you sleep for seven hours a night, you still have about eight hours left each and every weekday. Many of us mismanage that time. We spend it consuming rather than creating. We spend it numbing our minds rather than stimulating them. We spend it in the past rather than the future.[34]

Behaviour = Time

If you've got an hour for lunch, brown bagging from home can cut your mealtime to ten minutes. You just gained 50 minutes to read or listen to an audiobook while going for a brisk walk. Commuting by train or bus provides even more time for reading and studying.

These suggestions circle back to not quitting your day job to take the Brokering course. Once you are licensed, we will take a hard look at jumping in with both feet. We will map out how to fill those first file-free and client-free days. Getting started as a Broker, in my opinion, requires a minimum of 60 hours a week, so why not get used to that schedule now and invest

---

33 *Bold: How to Go Big, Create Wealth and Impact the World* – February 3, 2015 by Peter H. Diamandis & Steven Kotler

34 *RSA Animate Video* – "The Secret Powers of Time." The good news is that you can change your view; you have control over this.

an extra 20 hours per week, in addition to your current job, to get yourself licensed?

You also stand to benefit from staying engaged in your current job, especially if you are doing it with excellence and staying engaged with fellow employees. You want to be displaying a vibrant and energetic attitude; you want to go out with style. Do not be a downer about the current job you have; that will not serve you well mentally or otherwise. The people you work with today could very well become future clients and/or referral sources. I have watched a new Broker land client after client from his previous workplace. He never put the job down, never put the employer down and now he is invited back by management to give seminars on credit scores, first-time buyers, etc.

Be positive with your time, be laying the foundation now for the new work you will be doing. Imagine the hundreds of hours saved prospecting for new clients if you have maintained strong relations with all of those you currently work with.

Don't throw away those warm relationships. Don't think, "I'm leaving all you suckers behind; I'm out of here." View your current work environment as a building block, a cornerstone, of your new business and career. When you've moved on, you want former colleagues to remember that you were happy and worked hard to do your job well.

Avoiding distractions is critical in managing your time. Back in 1999, our family disconnected from cable TV. Of course by late 1999 everybody knew that all electronics would obviously cease to function at the stroke of midnight Dec 31. So we wanted to ready our children for a return to the 1800s. Of course I am kidding here, but the no cable TV years were a wonderfully productive stretch during which demand in our home for the latest toys plummeted. Stress also plummeted with the equivalent decrease in "evening news." Instead we read many more books; it was great. Books are like slow cooking, the healthy choice. Eventually, we succumbed to the lure of the idiot box, coinciding with a move in early 2004 and the corresponding upsell by the cable company during Internet connection. Ten extra dollars that cost ten extra hours.

Exercise is an equal part of time management. As contrary as it might sound, an hour spent exercising isn't an hour lost. Aside from likely extending your life, it energizes you for the rest of the day. You will be more alert and more productive. A stronger body leads to a stronger mind. You say you don't have time for the gym? The sofa sits on the floor and the floor is all you need for push-ups, squats, planks, etc. Do you need to burn up time driving to the gym and working out with a personal trainer? No. I do on average three hundred push-ups randomly during a week. If I'm watching TV—yes, damn you Netflix, this happens—I'll crank out sets of 20 push-ups periodically. A televised hockey game is good for at least 80.

Pen & Paper

Lists are a wonderful time-management tool as well, except when you clutter them with routine chores like picking up groceries and dry cleaning. Don't put 28 things on a list when you know that 23 of them are a foregone conclusion. I used to add all sorts of nonsense, just for that feeling of accomplishment as I crossed things off. Today when I create a to-do list, I first spend a few minutes asking myself two questions:

- Is it vital to my business, or can it wait until the weekend?
- Is there a way I can do this without leaving my office chair?

Only the no's to the above two questions make the list. It is a consistently short list.

This has led to greater use of Amazon, *www.sendoutcards.com*[35] and local couriers. Most recently, I have signed up for the app Guusto, which should allow for even greater gift-giving efficiency. I discovered this app during one of a few different

---

35 If you are signing up for *www.SendOutCards.com*, which you should be, you will be asked for a referral code. Please insert #172061 as this will assign your account to a wonderful person who has been a tremendous help to me over the years. I do not profit personally in anyway, other than the good karma. This is what counts most in life.

podcasts that I routinely tune into, specifically, I Love Mortgage Brokering.[36]

When you make a list, put down a maximum of five or six to-dos. They should be the difficult to-dos, the game-changing to-dos, the difficult phone calls you need to make, and the difficult meetings you need to attend. Crossing them off should happen in the first half of the day, and it will be meaningful as you do.

Most of us dread making cold calls, and so this activity goes at the top of the list. Start dialing. Learn to love it. Yet another new behaviour.

We are all given 24 hours in a day; if you choose to work for 14 of them, this is only acceptable if you are doing the equivalent of 28 hours worth of a regular person's work in those 14. If you are simply stretching out six hours of work to feel like you are working "hard," that is not acceptable. You need to be efficient and have endurance.

How long you spent at the office or on the road is irrelevant. All that matters is how much you accomplished, and how difficult the tasks were.

Mind you, if you are choosing to work a highly focused and productive six hours per day then I can respect that too.

36 *I Love Mortgage Brokering* Start with episode #1 and work your way through the series. There is gold in every single episode. Listening to the entire series would be a brilliant move for any new Broker, and it is a brilliant move for any existing Brokers as well. It is nearly as good as sitting and having a coffee with each of the individuals interviewed.

However Brokering remains a business that does not fit neatly into a six- or eight-hour specific box of time.

The key to all of this: be ready to commit to new behaviours.

CHAPTER 10

COMMUNICATION ESSENTIALS

"HONESTY COMPOUNDS. *It compounds exponentially. No matter what happens in your bank account, in your career, in your promotions, in your startups. Honest compounds exponentially, not over days or weeks, but years and decades. More people trust your word and spread the news that you are a person to be sought out, sought after, given opportunity, given help, or given money. This is what will build your empire.*"

— JAMES ALTUCHER

Basic Internet Protocol

No matter what you do now, or may do in the future, you must register your personal name as a domain name. Do it for me, please. But really, do it for you. It may not be too late. I believe the same goes for your spouse and your children's names. Claiming Internet identification for your name and any variations ranks up there in importance with getting a Social Security number and a driver's license. If you're lucky, your (web domain) name remains available.

For two reality TV Realtors who in their premiere episode spoke extensively about their myriad of "tech" connections, this message hit home hard when the third featured Realtor registered each of their personal domain names himself.[37] How neither of these two Realtors' personal tech connections had set either up with a website, let alone advised them to secure their personal domain names, brings into question just how tight their connections were. This seems not only like *IT 101*, but since the turn of the century, *Sales 101*.

Registering both yourname.com and, being Canadian, also yourname.ca is prudent. Take it a step further: does your own name have a unique spelling? Register the more common spelling too. Also consider registering something simpler if your name has a complicated spelling. A catchphrase with your first name, for instance.

Normknowsnumbers.com is perhaps simpler than *normstanaszlawszkimortgages.com*.

You should also Google your own name periodically. Just to see what others you share a name with are up to. It is also wise to add your own name to your Google Alerts list.

---

37 *"Million Dollar Listing"* S.F Ep1 S1 43-minute mark.

Email Address

If you are dedicated to the idea of becoming a Mortgage Broker, consider registering a domain with the word *mortgage, financing* or a topical word that speaks to the business. This creates perpetual advertising of what it is that you do. For instance, if you're involved with your kid's sports team, your email address is flowing out to potentially dozens or even hundreds of people and is speaking for you. Conversations, and subsequently applications, are sparked from my email address alone: dustan@ourmortgageexpert.com. It triggers questions about the market, and one thing leads to another.

Managing multiple email accounts is another layer of complexity and an opportunity to have a breakdown in communication. I limit myself to a single email address for simplicity.[38]

An email address based upon your professional domain name, rather than one based on the Brokerage house domain, has its benefits as well. As reticent as I am to ever have to move to a new Brokerage, one never knows what the future holds. Much like moving to a new home, switching an email address is a colossal pain and creates risk of breaking contact with clients, clients who want to give you their business. During my first three years as a Broker, my business email address was linked to the Brokerage where I worked. Naturally, I couldn't keep that email address when I departed. It was clever branding on their part and a subtle retention tool, as it proved complicated

---

38 For questions about this publication, please contact me via *dustan@ourmort-gageexpert.com*. As I write mortgages for a living, and this writing is my passion, responses may not be as instant as either of us would like. Staying focused on my clients is vital. This book has been a weekend project, and responses to inquiries will likely come on the weekends as well.

to update all past clients, especially those who had changed their own email without notifying me. To this day, four years later, the odd call will come in asking, "Hey, did you get the email I sent you?"

Choose wisely. And remain in control of your contact details.

One of the least professional things is an email address with a yahoo, live, Gmail, TELUS or Hotmail suffix. An applicant may be left feeling like they're emailing deeply personal and confidential documents to somebody's home computer on which their children may inadvertently be downloading who knows what spyware. The same goes for email address prefixes with juvenile nicknames, year of birth or worse.

Create a basic email signature as well. It is amazing how many realtors and Brokers end messages with "Sent from my iPhone," or worse, nothing at the end. Do you want to promote Apple products, nothing at all...or yourself? Have your full name, job title, phone number and website link forming a professional-looking signature for emails sent from any of your devices. Although my email signatures are not perfectly uniform across the board, they are complete. I'm working on the uniform part.

Email - Subject Lines

Change the subject line of an email every time the content of the conversation changes. This is a key day-to-day email practice to adopt in order to simplify your life. It conveys to the recipient that you are paying attention to the conversation.

It also makes it easier to find specific emails a year, or perhaps, 38 months later when you wish to verify, for instance, that you advised clients of certain policies or procedures like prepayment penalty calculations.

As an example, I title the first email to new clients "Client Agreement & Documents List." They might reply asking a question about mortgage portability. In turn, when I respond, I then change the subject header to "Mortgage Portability" and answer the question. It works the same with the lenders. If you're initially emailing about the "Smith file" and in the body of your reply you ask about the Brown file, be certain to change the header to "Brown file." It catches the eye of the underwriter and it's easily searchable months or years later. This is a habit to start forming when communicating with friends, family and current co-workers alike. It is one more way that you are conveying a new level of organization in your life.

You will also save every single email, forever. My current Outlook contains 162,000 sent emails and 186,000 deleted emails. Data storage and memory is cheap, so save your emails on at least two separate memory device(s) and keep them secure, ideally in a safety deposit box.

Contact Cards

Effective contact card management could be the most crucial piece of information in this entire book. It is a game-changer. This vital habit builds on the two new telephone habits presented in Chapter 9.

Building a contact card for every single person with whom you have any telephone, text or email contact, even peripheral (e.g., cc'd), is crucial to your future levels of efficiency.

When you receive a phone call from a first-time caller, an email inquiry from a new client, are cc'd on an email, or handed a business card, *you will instantly build a contact card for that person every time and complete it as thoroughly as possible.*

When a client tells me over the phone that their Realtor is Mr. X, at the end of that call, if not during, I am Googling Mr. X and confirming that I have found the correct person. I am then building a contact card for them and cc'ing them and the clients on an introductory email with my own contact card attached. Speed and attention to detail matter.

This has been one of my single greatest habits. It began years ago as something that just seemed natural to do, albeit with much less urgency at the time. Being able to scroll back through the incoming calls log on my phone, or through recently received emails, and in each case seeing all the individual names presented in a specific format is calming. In particular, it is calming on a day when you receive more than 75 incoming calls and now need to return one to that first-time caller from the appraisal firm, the lawyer's office, etc. You can quickly locate their data.

Your goal is to never see a random number displayed twice; each has a proper title. Even wrong-number callers. When a client calls me from a new number, I confirm the origin of the new number and add it to their contact card titled accordingly: home, work 2, parents, etc.

I also do what I can to complete all the fields in the contact card. I share with first-time callers my detail-oriented approach with contact cards (which of course hints at my detail-oriented approach to all things about their file) and ask if they mind sharing their last name, email address, perhaps even their place of work and job title. This is also giving me the basics with which to build their application.

When it is an incoming email, their email signature often provides the makings of a very complete contact card. This also allows you to answer a client's follow-up call from a position of strength.

In the notes section, add such comments as "referred by X," "working with Realtor Y," "working with lawyer Z," etc.

When you type the name of the client into the search bar, all contact cards with their name in the "Notes" section will appear. This allows you to easily locate the contact card for their Realtor, accountant, spouse, referral source, etc. This keeps things moving smoothly and quickly, and it avoids asking repetitive questions.

Each time you ask a person the same question over again your rating with that person falls, along with their confidence in your general abilities.

Another tremendous advantage this habit provides is a very

visual representation of your clients' origins. Because the name of the referral source is in the notes section of each client they referred, when you in turn type the name of the referral source in the Outlook search bar, it will bring up every contact they have referred you, ever.

This is also very important when you are working with Realtors, as you always want to be cognizant of pre-existing relationships five years later when that client calls you up again. You pull that client's contact card and ensure you do not put your foot in your mouth by dropping another Realtor's name. It is also good to take the temperature of that original relationship with the client. There may have been a falling out and you might need to be aware of this. Such a situation presents a good time to reiterate your commitment to client confidentiality.

For those of you who are competitive, at the start of this project in mid 2014, I had 4283 Outlook contact cards; nearing completion in August 2015, I stand at 6205. As of this reprint in May of 2017 my count has reached 8,572.

Social Media

Should you have a presence on LinkedIn, Facebook and Twitter? What about other social media outlets?

The answer is yes, a professional presence. Even your personal presence should be professional. Of course we all have real lives, with hobbies, quirks, funny friends, unique family members. I am not suggesting a scrub of your social media pages (although that photo of you guzzling a beer while behind the wheel of a jeep in the backcountry *before seatbelts were a thing* maybe ought to be deleted).

Create a detailed LinkedIn profile, refine (or create) your Facebook profile and lock your name down on Twitter, Instagram, Pinterest and any other social media sites where clients will inevitably research who you are and what you are up to in your spare time.

When it comes to posting on these various sites, I offer this mantra:

- **Is it true?**
- **Is it positive?**
- **Is it useful?**

If not, then don't post it.

LinkedIn is business-centric and requires a professional (in appearance) profile photograph taken in a professional setting. You must also take the time to build, and maintain, a complete an up-to-date profile. *Feel free to connect with me on LinkedIn for additional posts on the subjects of both Brokering and the mortgage market.* LinkedIn is like a forward-facing resume to prospective employers (i.e., future clients). There are regular updates emailed with the names of the people viewing your profile, who within days often call to discuss mortgages. Each time this happens it validates the medium. LinkedIn is a tool that is increasingly being used to vet the professionals we work with. Put yourself out there, professionally.

I have a personal Facebook page that is open to the public, and if you are into pretty well anything with two wheels then you might find my posts interesting. Facebook is, in my opinion, a snapshot of who we are once the suit and tie come off and the shorts and flip-flops go on. My profile is open, and if you are so inclined, feel free to friend me.

I also make use of a Facebook business page, which is designed to update existing clients, more than to attract new ones. I would be inclined to put greater effort into this tool were I not already working with such a significant client base.

Twitter I am less active on. There is @dustanwoodhouse, which is primarily directed at existing clients. Also there is @ourexpert, which offers Broker-to-Broker-focused content. Creating two different Twitter handles runs contrary to my views on two different email addresses. I am one person with one identity. And really is anybody paying attention to the one identity let alone a second? Admittedly, this is a piece of my own "branding" under (re)consideration.

I suggest refraining from posting or commenting on divisive personal topics through any of these platforms. When you get into religion, guns, politics or topics like children's vaccinations, all too often 50% of people are on one side and 50% are on the other. So whichever position you favour and share on Facebook or Twitter, you're potentially alienating half of the people, and of course once you start posting on multiple topics you will have soon managed to offend 100 % of your connections. Marginalizing yourself on social media rapidly marginalizes you in the real world.

Keep in mind that screenshots last forever and public shaming is the new online sport. There have been several very high-profile cases of people who were in fact extremely low profile up until that offside Tweet or post they thought was being shared with just "their closest friends or followers."

Ultimately, be sensible with your online activities, and hang around with people who are sensible as well. An unflattering photograph of questionable offline activities posted on the internet will live there forever. A thoughtless, insensitive, or rude post or comment will do the same. DO NOT EVER TYPE IN ALL CAPS! Doesn't it seem as though I just yelled at you? Sorry, no shouting on social media please. Also, never use profanity. In verbal conversation you might get away with the very rare use of profanity. However, in print it will paint an indelible picture of mental inferiority 99% of the fucking time. (See what I did there.)

Above all else, remember Internet rule #1: *the comments section is where intellect goes to die*. Restrain yourself.

Blogging

Mainstream media are heavily focused on the negative. That is what we humans crave, a constant stream of warnings of impending doom. Financial doom, real estate doom, celebrity doom, etc. Your brain will be better for your ignoring all of it. Yes, stay abreast of current events through reputable sources (books) in a cursory fashion (Google Alerts). But do not listen to hours of talk radio. It's junk food for the brain. It is the sugar, salt and fat of the psyche. We fixate too easily on all that might go wrong; this is not helpful. We have to re-train our brains to get rid of this bias towards what-if (bad) and adopt a mindset of what-if (good). Your mindset shapes your communication. So think positive to sound positive.

If you have a long commute each day then you must discover the world of audiobooks or the world of podcasts if you have not already. But again, focus on selecting positive content, content that will build you up and have you believing, as you should, that today is in fact better than yesterday and tomorrow will be better still. Books can be great sources of data for useful social media posts.

In the Mortgage Brokerage business, our clients are bombarded by negative media about the decisions they're making. Are interest rates about to rise? Are they going to be able to afford their payments? Are house prices going to collapse? Are they throwing their money away? There's constant fear around the process, and each and every decision they have to make. The client's amygdala is working overtime. So as Brokers we need to remain positive and calm. Be the steady voice, the rock for them to come to for relief.

You need to believe in what you are saying. Bone up on books that focus on the bright side.[39]

I filter my exposure to news via Google Alerts. I've created alerts for my family's names, my business's name, my

39 *The Rational Optimist: How Prosperity Evolves* - May 19 2011 by Matt Ridley.
Abundance: The Future Is Better Than You Think by Peter H. Diamandis & Steven Kotler.
The Four Agreements: A Practical Guide to Personal Freedom - Nov 1 1997 by Don Miguel Ruiz.

children's school and our community. Professionally, I receive alerts about Vancouver real estate, interest rates and the Bank of Canada, among others. I scan the headlines daily. I read fewer than 10% of the stories below the headlines. I stay informed yet limit my exposure to negativity and fear.

This steady stream of headlines is where I often draw inspiration for blog posts. All too often the rhetoric is lacking actual mathematics applied to it. There is little else like real numbers to deflate a hyperbolic headline about what rising interest rates might mean. I have written a three-part series this year (2015) built on previous posts and previous conversations spanning two decades titled "How I learned to stop worrying and love the bubble," which can be found at *www.dustanwoodhouse.com/blog*. This blog forms a large part of my communications with previous clients, referral sources and prospective clients. With topical and relevant posts you will keep people on your mailing list, and stay top of mind with them as well.

A blog is a serious commitment, sort of like a puppy. Posting has to become yet another new regular habit. Finding the time to spend with this new creature in your life is easy at first, but the novelty can wear off and the time can become a challenge. Few things look less professional than a website with a blog showing the last post as dated a year or more ago.

Better not to have one at all.

Texting, Snapchat, Facebook Messenger, etc.

These all represent informal methods of communicating. Messages between clients and I on these platforms tend to be limited to less than ten words and contain nothing material to a client's file, instead I direct clients to either call or check their email for a detailed response to their question.

There are desktop programs for texting, which at least allows the use of a full keyboard, but you need to be able to easily access a history of conversations in the future. You also do not want to have to be actively scanning multiple platforms for incoming communications from a client.

With so many avenues to go down these days, the best communication platform is the one you can most effectively access from any device and use to store the complete history of messages. For me, this is email. My clients are directed to telephone or to email. That is it.

If you take nothing else away from this chapter, please adopt the contact card-building habit.

It has been a cornerstone of my success.

CHAPTER 11

LIVE A LIFE OF LEARNING

Learning begins when the talking stops and the listening starts.

The average person types at about 40 words per minute. The pace of conversation ranges from 125 to 200 words per minute. However, humans can absorb data in excess of 400 words per minute.[40]

As such, the X2 button on the iPhone is a game changer. It ups the pace from approximately 150 words per minute to a more reasonable 300. The net effect is a 50% reduction of the time investment to get through the average book to four hours from the standard eight.

Each of us has four hours per week during which to absorb an audio book. Powering through a book per week, even a book

---

40 *Spritz* is a speed-reading app that has me pushing 400 words per minute within just a few hours of use. It is amazing.

per day during the weekend, is fantastic. Unlike television, there are literally tens of thousands of hours of inspirational, informative, and brilliant works to invest your time in.

Yes, we primarily learn by doing, and certainly, we learn from our mistakes. Reading allows us to learn from other people's mistakes. More importantly, reading allows us to focus on other people's success. Too many of us expend time, energy, and money trying to create a brand-new system, when simply utilizing an existing system to its fullest would have done the job just fine as it was. Learn what works for others, and adopt accordingly.

An excellent example is your website.

Most Brokerages offer an excellent template and reinvention is not really necessary at all.

However, when the time comes to design your own site, recognizing the value in retaining an expert in the field is important.

After a few years with the corporate site it was time for something custom. And with a $1,200 budget I achieved my goal.

Sure, a website is important, but I knew enough about the business, and about people to know it was little more than an electronic business card, it alone was not (and is not) drawing in new clients. New, high-quality clients come via referral, that precious transfer of trust. Search engine optimization and a big budget for Google AdWords will not draw high-quality clients. Knowledge draws clients.

Resources

Set up an account at *www.audible.com* and start absorbing the lessons of the successful people that have come before you. As you can tell by the variety of books I referred throughout, my focus is on non-fiction, peak-performance books. There are some excellent resources for quality reading lists such as Maria Popova,[41] Tai Lopez[42] and Tim Ferris.[43] All three are quality content curators, as well as idea generators themselves and well worth paying attention to.

From "The James Altucher Show" podcast, I have adopted the habit, not yet perfectly formed, of writing down (often emailing myself at random points) ten new ideas every day. Often these ideas form new topical blog posts. Mr. Altucher is himself an idea machine and almost any episode of his show is evident of this.

To distil the data gained through listening to 40,000+ words per week on a certain topic, I process and order thoughts through writing. Much of it remains in draft folders, waiting

---

41 Maria Popova's site *http://www.brainpickings.org/* began as a newsletter to seven friends and is now followed by more than five million readers per month. Wondering what to read next? Maria will have the answer.

42 *http://www.tailopez.com/* is a voracious reader and has a "Top 100" reads list worthy of your attention. Perhaps I was influenced by how many books on Tai's list I had already read, nonetheless this is a great resource and Tai is an interesting dude with a very cool business model. He truly has created for himself "The Good Life" as he calls it. Admirable.

43 I have been an avid consumer of all things *Tim Ferris* since his first book *The Four Hour Workweek* was released. *Subsequent books*, his *podcast* and the *TV series* all paint the picture of a man living an intentional life. Another great resource for finding the path to your own intentional life.

to be polished or processed, and as new books or podcasts enter my life, they allow me to refine and complete posts.

You can find Broker-focused content at *bethebetterbroker.com*, and client-focused posts at *ourmortgageexpert.com*.

To manage the mortgage process effectively, you need to be calm, confident, and knowledgeable. You must be able to answer questions on the spot or know how to find the answers quickly. Attending industry events is the best way to connect to the people with the answers. Collect their business cards and enter them into your contact database.

Industry events also provide an opportunity to chat with, and learn from other Brokers. I often walk away from a conversation and email myself a quick reminder to try a new lender or maneuver on a current client's file. I'm always learning something new because the industry is dynamic and the rules are always changing.

The industry offers regular trade shows, and lenders hold open houses and training events. Plan to attend them all over the first few years of your career. Getting to know who's who is vital to your future success. The better you get to know your lenders, business development managers, underwriters, and fellow Brokers, the greater confidence you will have in picking up the phone and asking them a quick question. Even a silly-sounding one.

Just as your confidence is contagious, so too can fears and doubts be. We all have moments of self-doubt; I have had many with the creation of this product in your hands. Vanquish them quickly, and keep moving forward towards a solution. Be cautious about whom you share fears and doubts with, as some people will only echo and amplify them. On a day-to-day basis once in this business, you will often watch a client's file head for disaster multiple times. Sharing these near misses with the client is of no use to them at all. Clients care about success: "Is it done? Are we approved?" being their primary concern. Focus on the positive; tales of the negative serve no productive purpose. Even a story with a negative start, that had a positive end, is to be avoided, as it still contains the negative.

Learning how to temper your communications and how to set expectations is crucial to keeping your clients calm, which in turn will keep you calm.

Learn how to communicate consistently and positively. Recently, I had a file in which the client was getting very concerned over us hitting the completion date on time. My message to allay his concerns at 9:12pm on a Thursday evening: "I am going to see to it that this file is complete on time through sheer force of will." We were up against some significant obstacles, and it took leveraging relationships with my appraiser, my underwriter and the lawyer's office, but it got done. Had I not conveyed that confidence the client may have scrambled to another lender and been gone for good.

The Social Side

In social settings the Mortgage Broker tends to be the one that people want to have work-related conversations with.

They may not want to talk about their work, but they want to hear about yours, often making inquiries about market rates or trends. Being well read and up to date allows you to have a well-worded response. Be on your game and know how to articulate the latest twists and turns of the market. Just as you are absorbing knowledge steadily, you will soon find you are dispersing it steadily as well.

This aspect of Mortgage Brokering has strong appeal to me. To oversimplify it:

1. Realtors charge a (justifiable) fee that leaves the clients (sellers) pocket.

2. Life insurance agents are associated with fees related to death and disability.

3. Financial Planners are telling us they can do better with our money than we can.

In other words all three of these professions want clients to give them money, a Mortgage Broker gives the client money. This seems to make a Broker a bit more popular and far less of a target for blame of any kind.

Faking It

When we are placed in an environment in which we have little knowledge, something as mundane as a Super Bowl party, the result is often one of two outcomes. Neither is great. Nerves get the better of you and you say something stupid or slightly off the mark enough so as to be memorable for many years to come. Or you find yourself doing a lot of polite nodding, smiling, and agreeing, which of course will come across as fake. Not good either. You may get invited back to the Super Bowl party next year either way after all, it is just a party.

But if you get caught faking it in the mortgage business, you won't be invited back. Know the language. When it comes to mortgages, it's not horseshoes and hand grenades. Close doesn't count. You've got to be precise in terminology and mathematical calculations.

Studying the language of the business and getting a grasp of the basic mathematical concepts will be addressed in the initial licensing programs and so will not be covered here.

Understanding how to use your mortgage calculator (often an app on your phone, or a program on your desktop) effectively and communicating with clients in a very detailed way is vital. There's no room for fudging numbers. Always take the time to be precise and demonstrate that you are detail-oriented and have a handle on what you are doing. This precision and detail is best communicated through email, even if it is an email to follow up the conversation. In these instances I prepare the email in advance of the call, working out calculations before dialing. This is partly to keep the call moving smoothly, and partly because I know that once I end that call I will be pulled in multiple directions and getting back to the ten minutes of preparing that email may not happen until much later in the day.

Case Studies[44]

Hello again,

Let's review the numbers one more time.

The payment on a mortgage of $300,000 at 2.64% over a 30-year amortization is $1,205.05 per month.

The payment on a mortgage of $300,000 at 2.59% over a 30-year amortization is $1,197.27 per month.

Now, your current lender (bank) suggests this is only a difference of $7.78 per month in payments, and pleads with you not to leave them for less than $8 per month.

I prefer, as you know, to be more precise in my communications and calculations.

Indeed, the payment difference is $7.78, but the real story is the actual interest expense difference, which is $12.37 per month. A bit more from your pocket. This is a trick of compounding interest and mathematics.

(Often a competing lender will say to the client that the difference is only $X per month. This is a fantastic opportunity for you to dig just a slight bit deeper and reveal to the client what lies just beneath the surface.)

---

44 Case Studies will form a significant part of the upcoming Volumes. At this point breaking them down and in particular explaining the language (amortization, rate, term, variable, fixed, open, closed, interest rate differential, monoline lender, etc.) would be largely superfluous to the goal of this volume.

So while payment difference is one thing, let's look at what giving up that 0.05% rate difference is actually costing you: $12.37 x 60 months is $742.20. I am not sure about you, but the extra work we have done to this point, and the remaining hour of your time to meet with the lawyer and sign the final documents, seems well worth $742.20 of after-tax money to me. (Added verbally but not in print: "I do not make $742.20 per hour myself, but let me know what you think.")

Also, you will recall from our very first conversation I suggested it is not all about the rate; it is all about options and flexibility. Your current lender, being a chartered bank, uses an Interest Rate Differential penalty calculation that could easily cost you four times as much as the prepayment penalty would be with the "non-bank" (a.k.a. monoline) lender we have this current approval with.

It is about more than rate, but in this case we are winning on that front too.

In addition, your current lender offers prepayment privileges that are limited to 1 day of the year and a maximum of 10% of the balance. When we initially spoke, you mentioned that you receive a quarterly bonus and would like to be able to throw $500 or $1,000 at the mortgage every few months. We have set you up with a lender that allows up to 20% cumulative prepayments in increments as low as $100 per week.

Also there is that $742.20 for another hour of your time. Let me know how you would like to proceed.

Kind Regards,

DUSTAN WOODHOUSE
REGISTER FOR MY BLOG HERE!
WWW.DUSTANWOODHOUSE.CA
AMP – ACCREDITED MORTGAGE PROFESSIONAL
PH# 604.351.1253
FAX# 1.877.797.8692

As you can see, the chapter on communication plays into this as well. But without having the knowledge around certain features of not only your own suppliers' products, but also those of your competitors, this would be a far less potent response. The detailed math is obviously a crucial component.

$742.20 per hour

Despite the comment above, you are looking at a profession where the power to earn $742.20 per hour does exist. As a Mortgage Broker, you've got the potential to consistently earn more than $200 an hour. There will be days you'll earn $1,000 an hour. The larger files are admittedly few and far between, and if you measured all of the hours invested in your career that allowed you to come up with the right solution for the client in such a short period of time, then it might look more like $1 per hour.

Nonetheless, you need to respect the earning power of this industry, but not ever let it be your sole motivation. As with 'rate' for clients, income should be number ten on your own list of priorities. By this I mean you need to realize that most people earning this kind of income have typically invested a quarter of a million dollars and seven to ten years in their education before earning dollar one. They are the Doctors, Lawyers, and Dentists. A group of professionals recouping the significant investments they've made in developing abilities to solve the complex problems. It's understandable why they charge what they do. You too need to dedicate yourself to having greater knowledge than you peers, which will in turn lead you to solving the files with greater complexity.

Crystal Balls

No matter how much you learn there are some questions that nobody is qualified to answer, and when the so-called experts try, they're often wrong. For nearly our entire lives, we've generally heard that home prices can't go any higher and interest rates can't go any lower. The reality in Canada has of course been the opposite. Prices have marched upward with only slight dips quickly erased when growth returned. Interest rates have declined to their lowest in at least 50 years with no sign of a significant upturn coming soon.

Clients are perpetually nervous and always asking questions along the lines of, "Is there a bubble?" or "What if the bubble bursts?" or "What if interest rates double when we come up for mortgage renewal?" So you need to prepare answers in advance.

Detailed answers that contain actual math and actual dollar amounts go a long ways towards positioning you as an expert.[45]

45 Many of these scenarios and the detailed answers trigger Blog posts. This gives me a compendium of examples at my fingertips. Sending a link to a 1200 word piece on a topic is far more efficient with clients than repeating the same thing over and over.

Learned Optimism[46]

Optimism itself is something one can in fact learn. There is science behind the claim, and there is anecdotal experience. If you are a negative-oriented person why not become the personification of anecdotal evidence in favour of learned optimism?

The doom-and-gloom crowds have been calling the Canadian real estate market a bubble for decades now. Their first mistake was assuming that the entire nation's market would be equally affected across the board by any one event. The "bubble-talkers" will always exist, always calling for a collapse in home prices, and no doubt will still be doing so long after I retire. The Chicken Littles expect that eventually they will be right, but to what end? So that they can themselves then buy a home at a "reasonable" price? The question is would they buy at any price?

I can't imagine why anybody would want to be right about such dire predictions. Economic and social devastation would result, wreaking havoc on not only the market, but also on the lives of many people. Calling for this "inevitable" and "certain" crash, as this segment does, seems to me a waste of energy. Odds are that the events of tomorrow will mirror those of yesterday. The only thing special about today is that we are each here to make the most of it.

In my humble view, everybody needs somewhere to live, even the Chicken Littles. Do they own themselves, or do they live

---

46 *Learned Optimism: How To Change Your Mind And Your Life* – E.P. Martin Seligman.

the virtues they espouse (of renting)? They often seem oddly silent on that topic. Sitting on the sidelines waiting for the "bubble" to burst simply doesn't make sense.

After all, a house represents much more than a financial investment for most families and people. It is a home, and home is where the heart is. House prices, interest rates and pushy salespeople are either secondary or non-existent reasons for why people buy and sell homes. The number-one reason is that *emotions drive decisions*. Are they getting married or divorced? Did they get a job promotion or were they fired? Are they having a baby? Are their children moving out? Are they downsizing? Retiring? These life events, and the emotions swirling around them, are primary reasons people buy and sell real estate in just about any market. Yes, there are stronger and weaker markets. But in either market there is always a level of core activity. More than enough activity, in fact, for a competent Broker (you) to earn a wonderful living.

There is no shortage of research done on the housing market, and just as the media will seize upon whatever they can for negative spin, I dig for stats that I can apply sound mathematics and logic to, in order to demonstrate the positive side of real estate ownership. You will find extensive writing of this nature in my client-facing blog.

Currently, the media loves to rant about the "debt-to-income" ratio, a ridiculous form of measure. It is like trying to use a yardstick to measure the weight of something. The real story behind this messy metric is far too complex to distil into a 15 second sound bite, and so it goes left untold.

In my experience, the notion that homeowners are maxed out financially is simply wrong. The bar is set quite high to qualify for a mortgage in Canada; it always has been. And despite stringent standards the majority of my clients still tend to borrow significantly less money than they qualify for. A few years ago, a survey found that 83% of Canadian households were comfortable with the equity in their homes. The survey also found that 77% believed low interest rates had allowed their neighbours to borrow too much money.

When I present these survey results to a gathering of a couple of hundred people, I advise everyone to look to their left and to their right. The people they're looking at are all, for the most part, comfortable with the equity in their homes. The same people staring back at you think you're overextended. That right there is the Canadian mindset: "Oh I know that I'm OK, but I'm sure worried that you're not." Of course, that person you're worried about is in turn worried about you.

When clients worry that interest rates may double, I do the math for them and put it in writing. I look at their mortgage balance and the amount of the payment they plan to make, and then calculate the ending balance at the renewal date. Then I double the interest rate for that new balance and show them what their new payment would be. I ask them to consider how much money they earned five years ago and whether what they expect to earn in five years would be enough to offset what they'd pay if rates doubled. I use this exercise to confirm that clients are comfortable with their financing in the long run. Most are shocked by the actual numbers, shocked by the lack of drama.

Here is an example of that math:

$300,000 mortgage @ 2.59% over 30 yrs. = $1,197.27 per month

5 yrs. down the road, the outstanding balance is down to $264,613.64

$264,613.64 mortgage @ 5.18% over 25 yrs. = $1,566.23 per month

Yes, this is a $368.96 per-month increase, but you have to ask a few questions:

Could you handle that size payment today if you had to?

Are you earning $368.96 more per month today than 5 years ago?

Should you be earning $368.96 more per month 5 years from now?

Do you truly believe that interest rates will double in 5 years?

There is also the option, though not desirable, of re-amortizing the mortgage to 30 years.

$264,613.64 mortgage @ 5.18% over 30 yrs. = $1,440.78 per month

This reduces the payment increase to $243.51

In addition, it is my personal belief that just as the federal government reduced maximum amortizations on insured mortgages from 40 to 35 and then 35 to 30, and then 30 to 25 years as rates fell, in turn as rates rise they will extend the maximum available amortizations back out again.

This could create yet another option, less desirable still, of re-amortizing the mortgage to 40 years potentially.

$264,613.64 mortgage @ 5.18% over 40 yrs. = $1,297.94 per month

We are now down to a $100-per-month increase with a doubled rate. Yes, the extension of amortizations is a poor solution, but it does keep people in their homes in cases where income levels have not risen, or worse, have fallen.

The bottom line: A 100% increase in interest rates = a 31% increase in mortgage payment.

As you can see, you are forced into learning an awful lot so that you can in turn present it clearly to your clients. But emails like these go a long way to calming clients, and a calm client is a happy client. A happy client is a referring client.

I advise clients on issues surrounding their financing. I do not comment on the property itself in very many cases. Advising the client on the correct property for them is the Realtor's area of expertise; financing it is the Broker's. Respect your Realtors and they will respect you.

In rare instances the choice of property may limit the client's lending options, and thus the potential resale options, such as remediated marijuana grow-ops, former drug labs or otherwise stigmatized properties. In these cases I will first have a conversation with the Realtor to ensure they understand the limitations on my side of the equation. At that point I will discuss with the clients why there are challenges with the financing and what that means for them now and down the road for potential refinancing or an eventual sale. But at no point do I say, "Yes, you should buy this property," or, "No, you shouldn't."

I Advise, Clients Instruct

Specifically, I advise on the topics I have been retained to advise upon, and am licensed and qualified to advise upon. I advise based on what I know, not what I think. Facts are more useful than opinions.

As Nietzsche stated: "Convictions are greater enemies of truth than lies."

Convictions and opinions are kissing cousins, and opinions can be formed from thin air; facts take work. Facts take learning.

Do the work, and reap the rewards.

CHAPTER 12

BE THE VAULT

There's nothing noble in being superior to your fellow men.
True nobility is being superior to your former self.

— HEMINGWAY

Be the Vault

In this industry, you must be the vault. A trusted repository of personal data. More important, you must convey to clients that you are a walking high-security vault. Start by becoming one now. A very human trait is the desire to gossip, or for some, to trash talk others; this is somehow a psychologically bonding thing to do with our fellow humans. Keep in mind that intelligent people understand that a gossip's nature is such that as soon as they are finished sitting with person A bashing on person B, they will soon thereafter be sitting with person B trash talking person A, C, D, and so on.

This is not a helpful reputation to have when entering this business. Better to be known for your discretion with sensitive information.

You will know more about clients than their friends or neighbours, and often their spouses, children and parents. Much of what you know revolves around their finances: credit history, net worth, income, spending habits and debt. There will also be personal information. You sometimes learn more than you want.

When a couple is separating, one of them may take a shot at the other. Simply listen and keep that information to yourself. Such comments aren't relevant to the transaction; they are not fodder for dinner table conversation either. My family understands that I will not speak about my clients with them, not at all.

I stress to my clients on the very first phone call that I do not share any details of their lives, financial or otherwise, with anybody other than their lender. I advise prospective lenders on things relevant to the client's mortgage approval. I don't give any client details to Realtors, lawyers, appraisers or referral sources. This much is a given for most people.

In addition to meeting these basic privacy expectations, I take it another step, and never drop the names of any client with whom I'm working. Not ever. If I get another applicant who works at the same company as a current client, I don't ask either if they know the other. For all you know you are making a connection that makes one or both of clients very uncomfortable. The same goes for working with two parties who have the same surname: I do not ask if they are related. It's nobody's business who I'm working with.

Client Who? Never Heard of Them.

If, for instance, I was an NHL player making $4 million a year and my Broker disclosed my name, I would be annoyed. While it may very well be smart tax planning or an investment strategy to have a mortgage at today's rates, the optics to the general public of a high earner having a mortgage at all would be difficult for many to understand. People might assume the worst, and so enters our friend gossip with its co-pilot, innuendo, once again. The fact is, wealthy people often have significant mortgages, with the capital deployed in far more lucrative investments, but yours is not to trumpet any information that might compromise your client in any way, shape or form. Start confidentiality at the root, their name, this is the easiest way to maintain control.

Do not be so presumptuous as to assume you know what constitutes a privacy breach in the eyes of the client. Instead always err on the side of caution.

Anytime you share a personal detail of one person's situation with somebody else, you have to recognize that the message you are conveying is that you can't keep a secret; specifically, you are not someone to be trusted with any personal details. Most of us have figured that out once we're out of grade school. We realize there is no such thing as a secret, but you need not be a part of one's escape.

Never Drop a Name

I've worked with clients who have encouraged me to drop their names. Some of these names are ones I would love to shout from the rooftop. Yet I hold my tongue. For all the clients who would not mind, there are far more who would, and these are the ones I worry about. If you are making exceptions, then it is not really a policy at all, is it? Also, there would be those who would question my motives and wonder if I might disclose *their* identity if they worked with me. My reputation is built on my being the vault. Sometimes too much of one, perhaps.

One evening I came home and found a bottle of wine with a ribbon and bow in our kitchen. My wife told me that neighbours from around the way had dropped it off as a thank you for handling their mortgage. She looked at me and said, "Really? You couldn't even tell me that you were working with our neighbours?"

My inner circle, on this topic, has room for just one. It's not that I don't trust my wife, of course I trust her with my life. It's just that talking shop is not a high priority for us and so it had not come up. I did not think to mention it.

This episode in turn played into one with even greater significance. We attended a barbecue with three sets of neighbours and during dinner one set casually mentioned to another that I had handled their mortgage financing. These neighbours in turn replied that I had also handled their mortgage. The timing of the two transactions was very close as well. Each was surprised that I had not mentioned anything to the other.

Later that week the third neighbour called me at work and mentioned that he hadn't initially been comfortable with the idea of somebody so close (geographically and socially) handling his mortgage. "But when we realized that you had acted for two of our neighbours at the same time and neither of them knew that you had, we figured we would be in pretty good hands."

The "be the vault" policy attracts more business than sharing clients' names with others ever could. The most powerful testimonial is one that a third party provides for you; you cannot give yourself a worthy testimonial simply through name-dropping. So let them talk about you, let them talk about how you never discuss them.

Privacy is paramount.

CHAPTER 13

MASTER TECHNOLOGY
ALWAYS ON!

*"Computers are incredibly fast, accurate, and stupid:
Humans are incredibly slow, inaccurate, and brilliant;
together they are powerful beyond imagination."*

— ALBERT EINSTEIN

Unplug the telex, toss those punch cards, and retire that pager.
Embracing new technology matters. As does your skill with it.

Of primary importance is your being easy to reach. You want
to have one phone number that connects whether you're
in your home, at the office, driving or on vacation. A single
number for clients to call is vital, and in this world of call
display you always want to be calling clients from a single
number—one they can easily call you right back on.

If you call a client from your home number, or your vacation home number, now they have that # as well. If you call a client from an internet phone, so that you can save $1.35, and it comes up on their call display as 'unknown number' or one with an area code from another Province or State there is almost no chance you will reach your client. You will reach their voicemail, which is very inefficient.

Your own voicemail must have a professional message that assures callers their communications are confidential and that their call will be returned promptly.

My one number is my cell phone, the same cell number I have had since I was 18. When at my desk for extended periods I could call forward it to a landline, but rarely do. The benefits of call display matter to me too. As does the ability to tap a pre-set text response letting the caller know I will be right back to them once the current call is complete.

Keep in mind that the same rules apply to an office landline phone number with an extension as they do to using a corporate email address. If you start promoting your landline and extension in your email signature, on your website and on your business cards you will have one more anchor holding you to that office. One day you might not be at that number any longer, but a new Broker will be. Likely a hungry one.

Time is of the essence when it comes to telephone responses.

The Hardware

The entire day is spent with a set of headphones (with mic) on, either Bose MIE-2S, which are discreet and very clear for both the caller and myself, or Bose Bluetooth over-the-ear headphones, which blocks out distracting background noise and also has an excellent mic. The key is hands-free for typing, i.e., inputting an application, looking up client data, with the bonus of avoiding muscle cramps in the neck. Having client voices in stereo is a huge advantage when dealing with thicker accents, as well as the inevitable low-talkers.

For email we have already touched on the benefits of a cloud-based solution. And of a single email address. Embrace the simplest solutions and utilize the technological advantages that are out there.

I don't have a laptop per se. And none of my portable devices hold any stored data; the data is only accessible through the cloud. All devices are password-protected in case of loss. All of the data can be remotely wiped from the devices instantly.

In your first two years of business, you should plan to be plugged in 24/7, operational through power outages even. Invest in an uninterrupted power source (UPS) for several devices: your Internet modem, the PC and a separate one for the monitor(s). Few events are as frustrating (for the client and yourself alike) as losing power while halfway through building a complicated mortgage application. Your client may be on a different power grid and waiting for answers about their file. Your excuse of a power outage is just that: an excuse. I've worked in a blacked-out office for two hours, UPS running the computer, and not even mentioned it to the clients at the time. Business as usual. Why add any stress or unrelated conversations when the situation isn't relevant to them? Focus on the clients needs, your own needs are secondary.

In order to always be on, you need backup plans.

Over time your professional life will come to revolve around your email inbox and your deal-tracking (Excel) sheet. This is not an industry for those who wish to apply the advice of some business coaches and productivity strategists who recommend putting daily limits on the time you spend emailing. That will be the death of your business. You must always keep an eye on your email or risk missing a question or challenge that could jeopardize a client's file. Delays kill files. Delays kill client relationships. Delays kill referral source relationships. *Time is of the essence when it comes to email responses.*

From the client inquiring about their file status to the underwriter working the client's file, most questions will be sent via email, and speed is everything. The faster you respond the better the impression you make. You must be *"always on."*

Make sure you have email access via your smartphone, and if you are taking a trip, make sure you have roaming sorted. And if you don't have it sorted then roam anyways, just pay the bill. Turning your phone off for a one-day trip to the US to save $43 in texting fees might cost you a $2,000 mortgage file. Be smart.

Set up email access through a tablet that travels with you and uses a proper keyboard as well. The responses you type on a phone are always more abruptly worded than those from a full-size keyboard. Few of us type as eloquently with our thumbs as we do with a proper keyboard.

On weekends, I now use an out-of-office alert. This was five years in the making though. Up until that point I was always on. The fact is I mostly still am; I monitor emails on Saturday and Sunday, and respond to urgent ones promptly. My out-of-office alert urges clients with a true emergency to call my cell phone. Very few calls come in over a weekend. A well written out-of-office response at least lets clients know that their email has hit your inbox, lowering their anxiety a notch.

When managing client file status, basic proficiency with Microsoft Excel is essential. In my early days as a Broker, I found Excel a better option than any of the client relationship management (CRM) systems offered. An Excel spreadsheet is simple to set up and allows simple tracking of key stats and data points. It also allows for easy uploading of historic data once you find the perfect CRM system. That said, learning and implementing a robust CRM system from day one is an excellent plan. Figuring this out prior to having dozens, or hundreds, of past client files to upload would be prudent. And there is no shortage of independent offerings such as Salesforce or Infusionsoft to name just two. Most national Broker networks have in-house CRM systems. The adoption of these in some cases creates the same risk as using the house email suffix. What happens if you must switch Brokerages?

Data is the foundation of any good CRM system; square one

can be an Excel spreadsheet with detailed client data and headings. Those with basic computer skills would be well served by taking a community class, or using a site like *www.lynda.com* for online tutorials on Excel and other Microsoft Office products. There are several features and shortcuts that will allow you to easily maximize the program. Whether your preference is a Mac or a PC, knowing how to use the technology to its full extent is important. Having been a PC guy all along and knowing that Brokering requires only the most basic of programs, I have not seen the need to make the shift to Mac, although I have allowed an iPhone and an iPad to creep into my life for non-work-related computing.

Mortgage Brokering requires little more computing skill than a mastery of your email program, web browser, and basic skills with the balance of the Office suite including Word, Excel and a PDF converter.[47]

One need not spend thousands on the fastest computer laden with the latest and greatest software. A Microsoft365 subscription comes with just about every piece of software you need as part of your cloud computing solution. As far as the hardware goes I cannot stress enough the importance of dual monitors. Keep tabs on email on one screen while using the other for mortgage application input, Googling or document review. Barely 15 minutes goes by without the dual-monitor setup demonstrating its efficiency. It is the key to operating in an almost paperless fashion.

47 I have used with great success "CutePDF Writer" for the past eight years or so. Google it, download it for free; it installs like another printer driver and is an incredibly useful tool on a daily basis in this business.

I am not a technophile, and I have no formal background in computing; even my reasonable typing skills are simply a by-product of doing. Whenever possible retain expert advice to accelerate your learning curve. Keep in mind that you are positioning yourself as an expert in your field, and protecting the do-it-yourselfer from them is a large part of Brokering. Don't you be a do-it-yourselfer as well. Take note of your own actions. Do not try to build your own website, your own computer, etc. Invest in experts and practice what you will be preaching.

Your shopping list:

- Bose MIE-2 headphones and/or
- Bose Bluetooth over-the-ear headphones (with mic)
- Back-up power supplies. Big beefy ones (modem, computer, monitors)
- A second monitor
- Microsoft 365 subscription (includes Office)
- CutePDF Writer converter

CHAPTER 14

MY FIRST 50 CLIENTS, AND YOURS

"Where do you get all of your business?"

This is perhaps the most often asked question by new Brokers of successful Brokers.

Naturally this is a hot topic in an industry where by some estimations, 65% of Brokers completed fewer than ten transactions last year.

Our own office processed ~170 files per year for four years running with just two of us, stepping up to 227 in 2014, which required the addition of a third, part-time staff member. Duties are split in our office with myself handling 99% of client interaction, my assistant (also a licensed Broker) handling 99% of lender interaction, and her assistant (also a licensed Broker) handling file details with lawyers, appraisers, payroll compliance, gifted housecleaning bookings, etc.

So where does all of that volume come from? In a word: referrals. *A referral is a transfer of trust; building trust with other trustworthy individuals today leads to new clients tomorrow.* Referrals flow from the mixture of habits and actions you have read about thus far, but there is more to it; much more.

Referrals flow from multiple sources. It's a broad mix, but let's look specifically at the origins of my first 50 clients and see what lessons we can take away from this list:

JUN 15, 2008

- Long-time client #1 from previous business   PURCHASE
- Close friend #1   RENEWAL
- Neighbours #1   PURCHASE
- Personal Accountant of 18 years   RENEWAL
- Close friend #2   PURCHASE
- Referral from Personal Financial Planner   RENEWAL
- Head office walk-in ***Friday 4:30pm   REFINANCE
- Referral from Personal Financial Planner   RENEWAL
- Long-time client #1/commercial transaction   PURCHASE
- Neighbours #1/2nd property   REFINANCE
- Referral from Personal Financial Planner   ETO
- Long-time client #2/commercial transaction   PURCHASE
- Long-time client #1/3rd property   REFINANCE

END OF 2008

The first thing to take note of is the variety of transaction types; this allowed me to gain experience that had additional depth and complexity, forcing me to ask questions, to think and learn. Each file offers you lessons that will pay dividends in future files. The key is to build not so much a list of questions and answers, as a list of industry contacts that you can call on for answers. (i.e. the lender representatives)

As you can see, my first six-month totals were heavily dependent on a single client. Equally as important, was my personal financial planner who also referred three transactions to me in the early days. Rounding out the bulk of the transactions was one set of neighbours representing two transactions. All but one transaction flowed from close friends or people I had done business with for many years. There were no random strangers dialing my number (despite various attempts to make that happen).[48]

All You Need to Know About Mailers

During my first six months I put together a presentable full-page coloured flyer titled "ten reasons to work with a Mortgage Broker" and mailed 11,000 of them every second Friday for six weeks to a targeted area in which I had spent the last 23 years of my life. The response was underwhelming to say the least.

A single phone call was generated: "What's your best rate?"

At the time I was too green to know how to manage that call and it ended rather quickly, without an application.

I had greater success simply suiting up and showing up at the office. The timing of being in that office mattered, mind you.

---

48 Much more will be said about the pitfalls of various marketing schemes in Volume 2. Let me save you thousands and thousands of dollars.

One Friday afternoon just before 5pm along came a random walk-in client (number seven) which was a $965,000 mortgage caught by just being in the right place at the right time. The right place? A professional office space in our Brokerage's head office. At a cost of $600 per month it was an investment in my business, it was worth every penny in the lessons learned from fellow Brokers and the assistance with completing these first 13 files. The right time? Being the only one still in the office on the Friday afternoon leading into the August long weekend could not have taught me a more valuable lesson. As per Chapter 8: suit up and show up!

JAN 2009

- Neighbours #2   RENEWAL
- Long-time client #3   PURCHASE

FEB 2009

- Close friend #3   REFINANCE
- Close friend #4   REFINANCE
- Previous Co-Worker #1   PURCHASE

MARCH 2009

- Client #4   PURCHASE
- Acquaintance #1   PURCHASE
- Referral from Personal Financial Planner PURCHASE
- Referral from Personal Financial Planner PURCHASE
- Referral from Personal Financial Planner REFINANCE
- Referral from Realtor #1   PURCHASE
- Referral from close friend #1   RENEWAL
- Referral from Personal Financial Planner PURCHASE

As you can see from the first-quarter results, my very survival continued to be dependent upon friends, and undeniably an incredibly supportive personal financial planner who could just as easily be titled "close friend" on this list. Despite my earlier comments about not counting on business to flow from professionals already involved in related fields, this relationship worked from day one, and continues to do so seven years later. The reason being that in 2008 few financial planners worked closely with Mortgage Brokers. There was no previously established relationship I had to worry about. In addition, our previous professional relationship had given us time to get to know each other and to respect how seriously we each take whatever we are doing.

At this point in the progression of clients we see the first tiny roots of a truly sustainable business taking hold. In the third quarter, with intense efforts, results of seed planting started to sprout. First, a previous co-worker with whom I had stayed in touch. Then a Realtor referral from an acquaintance, and two more people on the outer edges of my social circle. All these parties started to notice the significant time and energy I was investing to be the better Broker.

APRIL 2009
- Referral from Client #23   PURCHASE
- Referral from Personal Financial Planner   PURCHASE
- Referral from close friend #1   PURCHASE
- Neighbours #3   REFINANCE
- Referral from Head Office Staff   PURCHASE

MAY 2009

- Referral from Builder of clients #22 & 23   PURCHASE
- Referral from Builder of clients #22 & 23   PURCHASE
- Referral from Builder of clients #22 & 23   PURCHASE
- Referral from Personal Accountant   PURCHASE
- Referral from Client #22   PURCHASE
- Referral from Client #2   PURCHASE
- Referral from Builder of clients #22 & 23 files PURCHASE
- Referral from Builder of clients #22 & 23 files PURCHASE
- Referral from Head Office Staff   PURCHASE

JUNE 2009

- Referral from Personal Financial Planner   PURCHASE
- Referral from Personal Corporate Lawyer   REFINANCE
- Referral from Bank Rep #1   REFINANCE
- Return of Client #31   PURCHASE
- Return of Client #3   REFINANCE
- Referral from Builder of clients #22 & 23   PURCHASE
- Referral from Personal Financial Planner   PURCHASE
- Referral from Personal Financial Planner   PURCHASE
- Neighbours #5   REFINANCE
- Neighbours #6   PURCHASE

With a full year's cycle it becomes clear how the second quarter in particular is skewed towards purchase transactions. A statistic that holds true to this day. The second quarter tends to shift toward 50%+ of files being purchases, while the balance of the year most months are split nearly equally in thirds. Refinance, renewal and purchase transactions.

In the fourth quarter the progression of referrals from further and further outside my social circle continued.

Referral Sources

In many cases, previous clients became fantastic long-term referral sources themselves. Often these are people whom I never met in person. But I did do my very best for them, and that is what counts more than anything. A stellar client experience is the best marketing of all.

Even potential clients for whom I have not yet completed a transaction have also become very strong referral sources. This speaks to the interesting dynamic that surrounds personal finances. I have advised many people on restructuring a transaction, written letters with current market rates to help them hold their current lenders' feet to the fire, or referred them to other professionals (i.e. a Commercial Broker) in my circle. This builds trust in my ability to advise on the best solution for my clients, not the best solution for my pocketbook. I am thankful and respectful of the opportunity to advise, even if I am not the solution for that client.

Some of my best referral sources have long established relationships for their own financing, but may want a general second opinion. I do not need to intrude upon that relationship to feel successful. The focus should be to work on the referral sources personal file, it is simply to receive referrals from them—which is A-OK.

Often people close to you personally won't give you their

mortgage business because they don't want you to see their financial underwear. This is also reasonable. Take a moment to write out a list of people in your life that you would share your credit report, current income, assets and debts with. Odds are this is a very short list, as it should be. Now take another few minutes to think about why people you are not putting on that list should be putting you on theirs. Fair is fair. Keep this in mind if you're tempted to use guilt on friends or family. Such an approach will only alienate them, and cost you otherwise valuable referral sources or worse. Take the high road at all times. Take everything in stride with a smile and positive attitude. Prove yourself to be an expert in the field and promote your eagerness to share that expertise. Take what you are given, which if not their direct business is hopefully their referrals.

The New Kid on the Block

You're breaking into a business where many people already have relationships with a Mortgage Broker. Don't expect to burst onto the scene and break up those relationships easily, not with your zero years of experience. You need to be prepared to give something of value to win a client's business. Experts in many fields offer free e-books (a thing you might value) in exchange for your email address (a thing they value), and they do this to build a database of prospects around which they can expand their business.

Gaining a mortgage application will, in most cases, require

more than something so simple and impersonal. Although mortgages are far from simple, offering something like a free e-book on the topic of mortgages is unlikely to result in a mortgage application, much less a completed transaction. Many Brokers try to "buy business" via a $500 gift card in exchange for a completed mortgage transaction, or a referral that results in one. It rarely works. Five hundred dollars is not enough to inspire strangers to call another stranger and offer them all of their personal financial data. What will happen is that those Brokers will wind up handing out $500 gift cards to all the people who would have done business with them anyway, or worse they will not give this promotion to their friends or family, reserving it instead for "new" business. A major mistake.

Inevitably, your phone will ring and there will be conversations and meetings with potential clients that simply go nowhere, at least initially. But every time you talk with somebody about mortgages, you're planting a seed. It may take a few days or weeks or months or even years for that relationship to blossom. It depends on how high quality that seed is. Were they a warm referral? And it depends on how well you tend to it. Are you staying in contact? Were you knowledgeable, trustworthy and polite?

From your first day as a Broker the first script you will need is one that clearly explains your new career to people. Especially those you already know, your financial planner, accountant, insurance agent, Realtor, lawyer or notary. First you must be able to clearly articulate what it is that you do, what service you offer and what differentiates you from the pack. Only then will you let them know you are not so much looking for their personal business, but rather a referral if the opportunity arises. This puts less pressure on them, and it keeps things lighter.

Pursue these connections only modestly, if at all, before you're licensed. You may want to talk in greater depth about the business with a few people whom you trust and respect. Again, you're planting seeds, requesting help and expertise to guide you as you enter the business.

Sometimes new Brokers and new Realtors work well together because neither has established relationships in the business yet. Rookies who grow together stay together, often going through various "trial by fire" experiences, which makes for lasting bonds.

Realtors aren't typically privy to clients' finances. Individuals retain them to negotiate the purchase price of real estate. Buyers often tell real estate agents as little as possible about their finances. Clients are concerned that if they disclose they have plenty of money, then Realtors may not work as hard negotiating the price of the property. As a result, Realtors aren't always the ideal referral source, but if they see the value that you deliver they can be amazing supporters. Some Brokers swear by Realtors as the backbone of their business, others deal with no Realtors at all. I prefer a healthy balance.

Curiosity Feeds This Cat

I credit a large part of my success with curiosity about others, in particular the business they work at or own. When speaking with plumbers, gas fitters, contractors, auto mechanics, pressure washers, fence installers and others who are around our house from time to time, I ask them about their businesses. I'm genuinely curious about whether they're sole proprietors or incorporated, how long they've been in business, how many people they employ and whether they deal primarily with residential or commercial customers. In return, business owners often ask me about my work. If I wind up providing insight into housing prices, interest rate movements or pre-payment penalties, they may think of me when they need a mortgage. Almost every trade I have been involved with at our home has referred me to clients of theirs, and vice versa.

When appropriate I make the point that I choose to work with experts in their field, rather than to do-it-myself. This demonstrates respect for expertise (I just called them an expert), and tends to leave them thinking that the same logic might apply to their own financing (i.e., they should call me, the expert in my field).

You must continually prove yourself to be an expert. Demonstrate the courtesy to say thank you for referrals and the humility to understand why somebody might not refer you at all. This is not to say you should take no for an answer. Continuing to follow up with potential clients more than once puts you in a special class; follow up every quarter for a year and you enter an elite class: the persistence class. If you speak with people two and three and four times always looking for a way to contribute to their business and demonstrate genuine curiosity about how they run theirs, they will almost always find an interest in yours. Be curious, be persistent, but also know when you are being annoying and back off.[49]

Be a Referrer Yourself

When friends, neighbours, or clients ask me if I know of a quality plumber, painter, etc., I of course recommend the same trades I've used personally. I have referred some trades for decades with no expectation of reciprocity. This made clear from the start with these people that I build relationships on professional performance, not favours or kickbacks. For years, I was paying it forward and didn't realize it. You can start doing the same. Never ask what is in it for you. When one asks that question the true answer is usually, "Very little in the long run, that's what."

If you are not already referring people in need to a service provider with whom you already have a relationship, make another list of people you know, trust and respect that are in the service business and start to form another habit. The sooner you start, the better off both your friend the plumber, for instance, and yourself will be.

49 *Curious?: Discover the Missing Ingredient to a Fulfilling Life* - by Todd B. Kashdan

Educate, Don't Sell

I rarely ask prospects for their business directly. I know this runs contrary to Sales and Marketing 101, which teaches salesmen to be unrelenting in their pursuit of sales. I practice what I call education-based marketing. Feed people information that they're not getting anywhere else and they become hungry for more.

A book I read recently[50] really clarified and defined this education-based approach, which had seemed logical and natural to me all along. I had not really dissected it or thought too hard about it previously. I simply assumed this was how all Brokers positioned themselves. Indeed it is how all top-producing Brokers operate.

With clients and referral sources alike, I rarely speak specifically about product data; instead, I discuss market data. I may in turn weave product data into a narrative that includes a recent client's experience. The book I give credit to for crystallizing and further refining this method is *The Ultimate Sales Machine* by Chet Holmes.

When we, as Brokers, speak about rates, we are allowing the conversation to be centered on product data. If this is all you have to speak about, all you have to compete on, then all is lost. You can easily be beat on rate, if not by a lender then by a competing Broker. We all have access to the same rates.

---

50 *The Ultimate Sales Machine*: Turbocharge Your Business with Relentless Focus on 12 Key Strategies – May 27 2008 by Chet Holmes – Such a great book it gets another mention!

One way or another this statement is true, though some may dispute it.

That's why market data is the focal point of nearly all my conversations and blog posts.

Product data may well speak to root logic. A lower rate is better. Money saved today, end of story. However, few people are so linear and Spock-like in their thinking. In fact, Spock would review far more data points than just one. Actually, I am certain that Spock would be anything but a rate-centric shopper.

The data I am presenting to clients, often using real-life (anonymous) examples of previous clients to create a story with characters, is a mix of product and market data, a hybrid.

As I say, all of this is about planting seeds. Some take months, or even years, to sprout while others burst from the ground in just a few days. As a Broker, you're tending both kinds of seeds. You'll nurture some prospects for years. Others will bear fruit almost instantaneously. This is where some goal setting comes into play.

Make a Plan

Entering 2009 there was steady business from friends and neighbours; I easily could have sat back and called myself successful, but that did not enter my mind. I knew I needed to be planting as many seeds as I could, because the incredibly unpredictable nature of the harvest can create stress: stress in the office, stress in the home, and stress in the car commuting from one to the other.

My safety net, oddly enough, was not to retain a job while starting out; rather, my safety net turned out to be my social circle. These people were pivotal in my own pivot, to use the latest lingo. But how long was this going to last? One has only so many friends with so many mortgages. I was not going to wait around to find out, and that is what drove me to work as hard as I did in those first few years to establish new relationships, broaden my referral base, and expand my database.

If you are entering this business without the chance of a similar warm start, without warm connections in the real estate or finance arenas, then it is going to be all about the cold calls, and you need to have a very aggressive and disciplined approach.

For every phone call you make, a percentage of prospects will meet with you. A percentage of those meetings will lead to applications. The percentages will differ based on our strengths.

If you need to make 40 phone calls to arrange four meetings and those meetings lead to one application, and if one in three of those applications results in a file, then you need to make 120 phone calls a week. You need to drum up 120 names and phone numbers each week until you can rely on referrals from satisfied clients. Like in any other business, it's a numbers game. An excellent book on this approach to business is *How to Become a Rainmaker*.[51]

Of course, I like instant gratification as much as the next person. And talking about mortgages with anybody who would listen generated some of this early in my career. Once I even received a mortgage application from a person I met while waiting at counter at my local Starbucks. I often strike up a chat with the barista, asking them about their day, or if applicable what they are studying in school, etc. Being in a suit and tie they would often in turn ask what I did for a living. The one morning the person behind me overheard this three-minute conversation and something I had said about the mortgage business piqued their interest. They struck up a chat with me while heading for the exit; after speaking for just a few minutes, I heard the magic words: "No banker or Broker ever told me that before."

When I hear those words, I know they're going to become a client. We spoke by phone that afternoon. I built the application, by telephone as I do 99%of the time, and processed the mortgage shortly thereafter. This put a different (i.e., reverse) spin on "The Latte Effect," a term coined by Canadian author David Bach.[52]

Clients are all around you, just like good luck. You just need to keep your eyes and ears open. Perhaps plant a few clues;

51 *How to Become a Rainmaker*: The Rules for Getting and Keeping Customers and Clients – May 17 2000 by Jeffrey J. Fox

52 *The Automatic Millionaire*: Canadian Edition: A Powerful One-Step Plan to Live and Finish Rich by David Bach

business cards strewn about, the word *mortgage* in your email address, strike up conversations with others about what they do.

The point is that you will miss these opportunities if walking through life with eyes cast downward, ears and mouth firmly shut. It is all too easy to walk past a variety of wonderful opportunities. The superior alternative is to stride through life with your head held high, making eye contact, smiling and speaking with people. Business will stick to you all the way along.

CHAPTER 15

STRONG BODY, STRONG MIND

*"Sometimes the best thing you can do is not think, not wonder,
not imagine, not obsess. Just breathe and have faith that
everything will work out for the best."*

— AUTHOR UNKNOWN

Building a new career may mean building a new you. Without
question, running a high-performance business requires you
to live a high-performance life. There are many deadlines and
much to learn. I'm still learning, sometimes in the eleventh
hour, which can be stressful if you are someone who sub-
scribes to stress.

Stress, as with a sick day, is for the weak.

Mortgage Brokering is high pressure, with the government,
the lenders and clients alike routinely changing guidelines.
Sometimes Brokers learn of policy or rate changes in emails

sent at midnight on a Sunday night. Let's hope you submitted that application taken earlier in the day and were not leaving it to deal with until Monday. Not submitting the same day you get the application is not acceptable. You are beating a deadline that might not exist, but then again it might. And claiming that you did not know a change was coming is not an excuse. Change is always upon us. You lose. Stress builds.

Everything is Your Fault

When it comes to losing a file (and that is the correct wording, "you lose files"—nobody takes them from you), the only party to blame is yourself. You did not get beat on a rate, or beat on a product, or beat by the bank, or beat by another Broker. No, you lost it. It is 100% your fault. There are steps you could have taken, things you could have said, questions you could have asked, but you knew not what they were at the time.

Hopefully you can look back at your losses as lessons. In loss we learn our greatest lessons. Until you accept 100% responsibility and understand that everything is your fault, the lessons will be lost as well. Until you can be humble enough to realize that it was your mistake that cost you the file (your actions, not those of another) you will live in a shrinking world. I prefer to live in an expanding world. I make mistakes, I learn and I make fewer (or at least different) mistakes moving forward.

One of my mantras "everything is your fault," can be challenging to accept, yet liberating at the same time. If you adopt it too, then you are going to need resilience. For me my brain is most resilient when the body that houses it is getting fed, rested and exercised regularly.

Exercise

Agile minds are better equipped to handle these types of situations. Agile minds are most often found within active bodies. Your brain is an organ, and arguably it's a muscle that needs exercise as well. As does the body that is housing it. I may only workout for 20 minutes some days, but those 20 minutes will be intense. I'm like a pinball bouncing around the gym, working out non-stop, alternating between a push exercise, a pull exercise and a leg exercise. If you can't get to the gym, you can do push-ups, squats and sit-ups just about anywhere. Timothy Ferris wrote a wonderful book called *The 4-Hour Body*, which explains how to shave your gym time down to one hour a week, or four hours a month. To some extent I have adopted many of the lessons in that brilliant tome.[53]

Putting ten muscle groups under tension for 60 seconds produces a ten-minute collective workout. Allowing for some recovery time, you can have a meaningful 20-minute workout. As a Broker, you're going to get so busy with clients that spending an hour-and-a-half at the gym three to five times a week isn't going to be practical. Just as you look for efficiencies in work, you have to find them in working out as well in an efficient, focused, to-the-point process. It is possible to complete a 200-rep resistance workout in the time that some

53 *Tim Ferris*—mentioned more than once. A great curator of performance-enhancing data. Good blog posts, great podcast and always entertaining books.

spend adjusting their headphones, stretching, and warming up on the treadmill.

I have tried to shave the commute time out by exercising at home, but this is not always effective or practical. The ritual of going to the gym is an important part of the habit. I turn the commute into productive time by listening to an audio-book during the drive, and often the workout too. Shifting away from music while pushing weights took a long time to adjust to, but it was worth it. The truly effective multitasking opportunities are few and far between. Feeding the mind while building the body is one such chance.

Rest

I engage in a form of meditation nearly every afternoon around three o'clock. I take a nap. I don't fight the natural tendency towards afternoon lethargy. My body and brain are telling me they're tired, so I listen. Wasting even more energy resisting is not prudent. This break is also highly ritualized as well. It's 20 minutes long, rarely more than two minutes shorter or longer. I don't always sleep, but rest with the lights out, eyes closed, calves elevated on a chair, back flat on the floor with no pillow. I keep a yoga mat under my desk, and try to remember to lock the office door. I focus on long, deep breaths, on clearing my mind, trying to count each breath down from ten without allowing another thought to intrude. A calm mind is the goal, and almost always I am asleep within seconds. It is amazing how many times I awake with a solution to a complex problem from the morning all mapped out. This session allows the brain to collect and sort all of the data absorbed during the first part of the day and shift it from the RAM to the ROM. Sort of like backing up the first half of the day's events onto your internal hard drive. Without question it improves (my) long-term memory.

Immediately following the nap, try to take a 20-minute brisk walk around the block. Put on your hands-free headset and make a few calls to friends, family members or co-workers. Specifically to people who will neither expect you to be sitting in your office nor have a question for which the answer is sitting back in your office. There are many conversations better had without the distraction of the office electronics. This is like a natural stimulant and negates the need for those two or three cups of coffee that others opt for. These 45 minutes or so of downtime will give you a boost that allows you to power through the next seven to nine hours with energy and enthusiasm. Whether your goal is to work a productive 14 to 16-hour day, or simply to be focused and attentive for the six hours or so in the evening following a nine-hour workday, this program will help.

Fuel

The brain consumes 20% of the energy you burn each day. It is a power-hungry device, and what you fuel your body with is what you in turn fuel your brain with. As they say, garbage in, garbage out. In a quest for clearer thinking, my own dietary habits have been shaped as much by seeking performance foods as by circumstance (Celiac). One tends to pay little attention to precisely what they are ingesting until some external force dictates its importance. My forced detailed review of ingredients since 2008 was the catalyst for taking things a step further. I have picked up various dietary modifications over the years, including chia seeds from the book *Born to Run*,[54] hemp hearts from a co-worker, grass-fed butter and MCT oils from Dave Asprey,[55] and various other tweaks based on tips from podcasts by both Ben Greenfield[56] and "The fat burning man."[57] If you are not tuning into guys like these for ideas, at least tune into the ingredients of what you are eating.

The collective influence of these various sources has led to some profound changes for me. Including taking a year off from alcohol (One year that turned into 2.5 years, and counting, as of this July 2017 update). I will not get on a soapbox on this topic other than to say that the personal benefits have been remarkable. Greater mental clarity and energy kicked in at about six weeks from the elimination of the admittedly small amount of drinking I used to do. I never would have thought a few drinks per week mattered, but then again from another perspective the absence of a few drinks per week just doesn't matter either.[58] The motivation for this decision could

54 *Born to Run: A Hidden Tribe, Superathletes, and the Greatest Race the World Has Never Seen* – Mar 29 2011 by Christopher McDougall– An inspirational book for those interested in pushing themselves a step further.

55 *"The Bulletproof Executive,"* an excellent *podcast* hosted by Dave Asprey, a man all about pushing cognitive function to new levels. A true bio-hacker with a series of great guests and fascinating topics aimed at building a better you.

56 Ben Greenfield hosts another podcast with unique guests and topics that challenge the status quo. Lots of great takeaways here, and he's also an amazing athlete.

57 Abel James is the host of the podcast *"Fat burning man,"* which is also a great source of dietary and exercise advice.

58 James Swanwick wrote an excellent post that was the catalyst on the morning of Oct 6th, 2014 for this decision. Find him on Facebook.

be categorized as "effective time management" with fewer evenings spent fuzzy, and every morning a sharp one as well.

Engaging in activities that sap energy and clarity in the moment, as well as the next day, does not align with the path of a top producer, or with somebody trying to master a new career. When one drinks too much at a party, or worse at a work function, people notice, and as we discussed earlier, everybody talks (and posts). In this case they will be talking about you the next day, not always favourably.

As a Mortgage Broker, your reputation matters. You are trying to convey an image of intelligence and confidence that invokes trust. Being *that guy* or *that girl* from the event the night before is not helpful.

In simple terms, considering today's laws with regard to driving under the influence, if you must drink, limit yourself to one when no food is present, perhaps two with a meal.

Keep in mind that alcohol brings few if any benefits to work-related settings; more often than not you will see it bring about for at least one attendee an indelible negative impression.

More than a few wise people can tell you that free drinks are often the most costly drinks of your life. When attending professional events and conferences, be professional. Act as though you're meeting your future in-laws for the very first time. Make a good impression. As I often say (to myself), "Make smart choices."

You can easily go stealth. Drink pop with a wedge of lime, or cranberry and soda, and no one's going to ask you if you're drinking or not. If you feel as though you need an excuse, simply state that you are driving, or have to leave early to get the kids to school.

When making a commitment to a new career, make the same commitment to a new you on some level. Whether it is aming up the level of physical activity in your life, or dialing down the level of late-night schmoozing and boozing, such decisions and actions will once again reinforce the positive change you are making in your life to those around you. They will trigger conversations and admiration for the positive results. Few people commit to change, and fewer still stick to it. We are all impressed by marked change in others though. As much as negative changes can act as a social repellent (rightly or wrongly), positive change attracts and impresses.

Embrace change.

CHAPTER 16

FRONT AND CENTRE

"Change your thoughts and you change your world."

– NORMAN VINCENT PEALE

Perhaps there was a time when it was cool to sit at the back of the room, but being cool is not really all that life is about. What is cool is being attentive to your surroundings, being engaged with others, and learning. Learning happens in the front row.

Earlybird

Be the first to arrive and the last to leave. That's my advice for attending conferences and seminars. And when you arrive, do not park nine blocks away to save $3. Pay the $20 to the doorman (most conferences are held in hotels) for parking. Once there, stay until the very end, as every minute is another opportunity to meet somebody new, right up to the point when you're waiting for your car to be brought around. Linger until they turn out the lights. (In a social way, not a creepy stalker way)

Invest in People

The $20 paid for premium (valet parking) service can yield premium results. Aside from putting you next to the other people willing to pay a premium for a quality service (a desirable client profile), it also puts you front and centre with some of the most outgoing staff in the hotel. Let me offer an example where this $20 investment has returned itself a thousand times over.

In the summer of 2009, I spent $500 for a booth at an event sponsored by the Vancouver Board of Trade. The event itself yielded nothing useful directly; however, after the event the doorman who retrieved my vehicle (not his job per se) said, "So you're a Mortgage Broker?" He had seen my business cards on the console (kept there by design at this point). He was currently enrolled in the "Life Licensing Qualification Program" (LLQP) himself and was going to transition into the role of life and health insurance agent.

We had a brief conversation and he suggested that we connect for lunch. To his credit he followed up a few weeks later with a phone call. To my credit my call display showed his full name and workplace as I had diligently input his contact details that first evening we met. We scheduled a lunch, which was the first of many. Even before he became fully licensed, the referrals began with his co-workers. Six years later, we still refer clients to one another. Although for the first year or two I was unable to reciprocate as I had a dedicated referral relationship with my own personal CFP, this man continued to forward clients my way. I believe he did so for two primary reasons: my reputation is for fast response (making the referral source look good) and for tenacity in getting the job done. This gentleman had a long-range view. He knew that eventually there would be an opportunity for me to send him clients.

The opportunity came two years into the relationship when my own CFP's book of business grew so large that he asked that I be more selective of the clients I was referring to him. And so began the reciprocation on my part to this now established contact. That chance meeting, and the dedicated follow-up on both our parts, has produced a productive relationship that continues to work to this day for both of us.

How many $20,000 conversations do we miss out on each year? Go the extra step.

Front Row

When you attend presentations always sit in the front row. Eye contact with the presenter demonstrates interest in what they're saying. One side benefit of being in the front row is that you are unlikely to nod off; joking aside, there is little doubt that we pay less attention to the speaker and more to our Facebook feed when we sit at the back of the room. If you are going to pay good money, and take time out of your day to hear somebody speak, then do them the courtesy, and yourself the benefit, of paying attention. Whether you arrive early, or ironically even when you arrive a few minutes late, there are almost always front row seats open.

Those in the front row usually get their questions answered and are often able to meet the presenter afterwards to ask a few follow-up questions. Most presenters welcome feedback. You may want to follow up with a phone call or email a few days later if you see the potential for a business relationship or at least an opportunity to refer their services out to others. At the least, if you enjoyed their content, connect with them via the various social media sites and pay them a compliment when you can.

Carpe Microphone

In the fall of 2009, about eight months into my membership with a Vancouver real estate investment club, the Real Estate Action Group,[59] I was sitting in the front row when an opportunity came along that might have made some cringe. The group's in-house Mortgage Broker was absent and rather than go without any sort of mortgage update, the host of the event, Ozzie Jurock,[60] noticed me in the front row and (in a room of 200 real estate investors) asked me on the spot if I would be so kind as to get up and give a quick synopsis of what the month looked like as far as interest rate movement, etc. I did not miss a beat, at least that's how I recall it, and jumped up and grabbed that microphone.

---

59 *The Real Estate Action Group: http://reag.ca*

60 *Ozzie Jurock: http://www.jurock.com*

Within a few minutes I learned another valuable lesson: few things validate an individual like a microphone.

Anytime you have an opportunity to speak to a group, seize the opportunity and demonstrate that you're an expert at your craft. Knowing your stuff is critical to mustering the confidence to speak publicly—it really is the only requirement. Most of us can recall the horrors of grade school and our teacher calling us to the front of the room to answer a question, or worse, give a presentation. But so much of this fear isn't rooted in the speaking so much as it is in the fear of getting caught not knowing what we are speaking about. When answering a question or giving a presentation on a topic that we know inside out, the process is always much easier. So be prepared, and know your stuff!

No doubt, sweaty palms and dry mouth go hand in hand with public speaking. Groups such as Toastmasters have helped many calm their nerves. Toastmasters provides a safe and constructive environment for people willing to admit they're nervous about speaking publicly.

First Learn, Then Prospect

My motivation for joining this particular real estate investment group (REAG) was specifically to absorb real estate data, not to troll for clients or brush up on public speaking skills. However, the pursuit of education led to the opportunity to speak that one evening, and at least once per year subsequently, which led to greater validation, and over the following months and years several client applications. This was an investment in myself that took time to pay dividends, but once again has far exceeded the initial investment.

To date 64 new clients have flowed through the web of connections built through attendance at 10 to 12 Real Estate Action Group meetings per year.

In an industry where the median Mortgage Broker processes ~24 transactions per year, to have an average of 12 per year originating from a monthly meeting is remarkable. To be fair there was zero business flowing from this over the first 18 months. It took time to get traction.

More meaningful than the easily defined metric of transactions has been the wonderful web of social interactions. Lasting friendships have been formed and great times have been had outside these meetings as well.

The moral of the story: **take action.** (As Ozzie would say, "be a human doing, not just a human being)

Such investor groups exist all across the country. Seek one out. Join for the education. Do not give up on attending after just a few meetings because you have not picked up a new client...at least not if you are taking away valuable information. Budget for two years of membership before you do get an application from such a group. Simply focus on absorbing market data and being a constant presence. Watch for opportunity, and when it presents itself do not hesitate. Seize it.

Once you're licensed as a Broker, you may also consider

joining a Business Network International (BNI) group. These groups offer similar opportunities, with each meeting giving you the opportunity to deliver a 60-second elevator speech to a group of up to 30 attendees. BNI is a safe place to build confidence and connections. It also helps you weave yourself into the fabric of the local community.

Someone who has lived in the same community for 30+ years (as I have) may not find BNI as useful, as you may have an established network of professional connections with whom you have done business and know personally. Take the time to write out a list of all the people and their professions that do already exist in your network. Are you doing all that you can for these people? Can you do more? Meet one or two of them each week for breakfast, especially as you work into this new career. Maximize, or at least enhance, your existing network before you try to build a new one from scratch.

Mortgage Brokering is a game of chess, not checkers.

Always play the long game.

CHAPTER 17

DON'T SET GOALS, SET DEADLINES

"Arriving at one goal is the starting point to another."
— JOHN DEWEY

A goal without a deadline is just a dream. Saying you want to become a Broker is a dream with vague hope for success. Saying you will be a licensed Broker working for X Brokerage by Y date—that is a goal defined by a deadline.

Pen & Paper

Writing down goals in a journal, often just before bed, has

worked magic for many. There is something special that happens in our brains when we put pen to paper. It can clear our heads or at least free up enough space for solutions to arise to complicated problems. Often the very next morning. I've found that writing down goals and assigning a deadline to achieve them creates a realistic expectation. It becomes that much closer to reality once in black and white. Talk is cheap and forgettable.

While I am a fan and a user of the app "5 Min Journal,"[61] the digital versions of journaling feels more like a sound bite than the core story, but it is still a useful tool. *Winstreak* is another app along the same lines. A quick hit of positive reinforcement, a record of conversation starters with a friend or family member. The ability to include a few photos taken during the day with the comments uploaded to these apps is also cool. While these apps are important and useful, they are akin to a protein bar between meals, they are a good supplement but the main course should always be some time spent with a notebook and a pen.

Part of a good night's sleep is avoiding digital screens for a solid hour before bed; this is one more reason to write your journal in the evening with a pen and notebook.

Most day-to-day business can be summed up with, "If it isn't written down, it didn't happen."

---

61 *The Five Minute Journal: A Happier You in 5 Minutes a Day.* I use the app, although you can order a hardcover version from creators Alex Ikonn & UJ Ramdas.

With regard to goals, I suggest this instead: "If it isn't written down, it won't happen."

Take Action

Signing up for the Broker's course is just the first step. Your deadline for signing up, if you have not already set one, should be within one week of finishing this book. You either will or you won't, so write down your decision.

Once signed up—which, having read this far, you likely will be—set deadlines for completing the assignments. Your goal should be a minimum of one assignment per week; two would be better. Do the math, i.e., 20 assignments means 10 weeks of work prior to registration for the exam. Stick to your written plan.

As for taking the exam, results might take another week to post. What happens on the day that you pass? You need to keep momentum; you need to keep mapping this out. You will have already written out a list of contacts in the industry from whom you can request guidance, assistance or even interviews. From the date you pass, your next deadline is interviewing with at least three Brokerages within the following ten days.

Preparation for the exam in British Columbia consists primarily of a correspondence course, with optional classroom sessions. Attend all supplemental sessions offered, which is typically during the weekend or workweek evenings. I attended all of them, and a few twice due to an overlap in the scheduling. I met people taking the course for a second or third time, not because they had failed to complete the course assignments, but because they had failed to set a date to take the exam.[62] A full year of momentum lost, of time, lost. Also another $1,000 to sign up again, another two to three months' delay to complete assignments. Time wasted, money wasted, all due to a lack of self-imposed deadlines.

Document Your Plan

I had specific goals in 2008; starting in early June left nearly seven months with which to work. And work I did. My goal at that point was to average one completed file every second week and to intake at least one new application per week. Intake of applications is often done via a "pre-approval" conversation. (The nature of a pre-approval and all that it is and is not will be its own chapter in Volume 2.) Pre-approval applications can take months, sometimes years, to "go live," or in other words to generate actual revenue. However, they are an excellent way to refine your scripts and hone your skills with client interaction.

Although I fell short of my goal by one completed file, it was still a strong enough launch to be awarded the "Rising Star" at the Brokerage's annual gala.

A few weeks into 2009, my first full *calendar year* as a Mortgage Broker, my manager asked me to join a small group for a goal-setting exercise. She provided a template for projecting

---

62 In BC you must retake the course if you fail to take or pass the exam within one year of completing all of the assignments.

our earnings by year-end based upon the average commission per file.

We estimated how many files we'd need to complete over the year and then, adjusting for seasonal slowdowns, estimated a monthly total. We also adjusted for our start halfway through January.

I set a rather lofty income goal of $160,000 for that first year. Although I press the point repeatedly that one should not enter the field of Brokering simply "to make a lot of money," the fact remains that a lot of money can be made in the field of Brokering.[63] With 13 files behind me I had an idea of what it took time-wise to complete a file and was enjoying the work itself. Extrapolating the number of files out that seemed reasonable to complete in a year brought me to this income amount. There was, I admit, an accumulated debt hangover from my previous business that needed to be addressed. It added pressure to perform. Being the sole breadwinner in our family was another layer of pressure.

Although this income goal exceeded my income total for the previous four years combined, it was clear to me that it could be achieved. A Broker with seven months' experience could replicate that success today, and it is my hope that several

---

63 *Stats Canada excerpt*: According to the 2011 NHS, 10% of Canadians had total incomes of more than $80,400 in 2010, almost triple the national median income of $27,800. To be in the top 5%, Canadians needed to have a total income of slightly above $102,300 and to be in the top 1% required just over $191,100, nearly seven times the national median income. The top 10% of Canadians made an average income of $134,900, with the top 5% making one-third more ($179,800) and the top 1% almost triple that amount ($381,300). Meanwhile, the bottom 90% had an average income of $28,000.

readers of this will do so. The year 2009 was the only year I set an income-related goal. Since then my goals tend to be related to happiness of clients, satisfaction of referral sources, efficiency ratios, total volume of files, etc. The income side of things tends to take care of itself.

When setting this goal in 2009,[64] average commission was estimated at $2,000 per file. I worked out the number of files I'd need to complete each month allowing for seasonal market differences, as well as how many applications it would take to obtain a single "file-complete."

"File Complete": the magic words that both clients and I want to see in print.

I kept working the numbers backward, estimating how many phone calls would be required to draw an application. If it took 15 calls, it might also require several meetings, coffees, lunches and dinners to attract the applications. At the end of this goal-setting exercise the work that I felt needed to be done led me to 80-hour workweeks, a pace maintained through the first few years, perhaps the past seven. This is reflective of my approach, which is to underestimate the rewards, over-estimate the work involved and budget accordingly. I like to work both smarter and harder.

Reality Check

Around March 2009, a friend called, inviting us to attend his

---

64 Was there some sort of economic event in 2009? One that should have had me giving up? Uh-huh. Create your own economic event!

40th birthday party in Las Vegas. I told him my family wouldn't miss it, then hung up and asked myself how the heck we would pay for that trip. Although I was finally earning, it was still early, and I was putting most of it back into the business in the form of memberships to industry organizations and registration for seminars and conferences. What remained went to household bills and reduction of debt.

Going backwards and deeper into debt for a trip to Vegas just didn't add up.

Our family loved road trips though. I convinced myself we could afford the trip by driving, rather than flying, and staying in a $70-a-night hotel 6 miles up the Las Vegas strip. So here I was, the "rising star," apparent envy of other rookies, scrambling for gas money and charging a $70-a-night hotel room in the desert to a credit card only just brought below its limit.

This was one of the more difficult, yet brutally honest, stories I shared with those 1400 mortgage agents in the previously mentioned 178-slide presentation series. It exposed a bit of a double life, which is reasonable, as most of us have some skeletons in our closet, some still twitching. The trick is in not letting them weigh you down and define who you are. I always knew we would power out of that slump, and at that point I knew we had found the way and we just brushed the limits one last time. The point is you just never know what's happening in people's lives. Even though I was successful on paper, behind the scenes things were tight. I worked hard out of necessity. I mapped out 80-hour weeks because I was on a mission.

Today, I work hard because I love what I do.

Success did come, but not without preparation, setting goals and following through. I was curious to learn, eager to meet new people and willing to break habits that were detrimental to my performance and form new habits to increase my performance. All of this made working hard a little bit easier.[65]

As such, in 2009 things came together faster than I had planned. My goal of 80 files was hit in early September and the year ended with 108 completed files. Still working solo, I had blown past my own expectations and those of the industry, once again accepting an award for top producer at my Brokerage's annual awards gala, boosting my confidence and belief that my family's financial future was at long last looking brighter.

65 *59 Seconds: Change Your Life in Under a Minute* – December 28, 2010 by Richard Wiseman. Written by a self-professed "anti-self-help-quackery" gentleman, this book is filled with practical guidance for a better life.

CHAPTER 18

CREATE RAVING FANS

"One of the marks of successful people is they are action oriented. One of the marks of average people is they are talk oriented."

— BRIAN TRACY

It is Not About the Money

Focusing on how much money you want to make is no guarantee for success. In fact, over the long term it may impede your success. You may be reading this and saying, "Hang on, the last chapter outlined a direct income-related goal?!" and you would be correct.

That goal was based on extrapolating what had been accomplished in the previous seven months and building upon it to achieve maximum efficiency. That income figure was not the basis for becoming a Broker.

A vital point to make is that on a file-by-file basis I never let the specific commission enter the picture; I never once pre-calculated what I would be paid on a file. I also never wavered from pre-paying for all of my clients' appraisals from day one (in my market 99% of direct lender competition will do the same). I never let on to clients that my life was as financially tight as it was. My issues are just that—my issues. Clients have their own issues, and their issues are all that matter.

Another distinction is that income is just one way to keep score. However, the primary goal from which that 2009 target number flowed was to end the year with 80 satisfied clients, 80 raving fans in fact. Scrolling back through the list of 2009's 108 clients, I can say "mission accomplished" as 99 of them have since referred a new client or returned with additional business of their own. A 90% "retention rate." Of course we would all like 100% of our clients to either refer or return to us, but 90% is a figure on which one can build a successful career and business.

Focus on Client Solutions

The highest priority of any business should be to provide a service that people need. To provide solutions to existing problems. People will want to work with you personally only if you are an informed and trustworthy solution. The resulting income is simply a by-product of that trust.

One of my favourite lines from Simon Sinek's *Start With Why* says, "I'm better today than I was six months ago, and I know that six months from now I'll be better than I am today."[66] At least once a week since reading it, that quote goes through my mind. I use this as a tagline on my email campaigns. It's an overt apology. It says, "If I've done something wrong, I'm sorry, but I'm trying to improve and I hope never to make the same mistake twice." It's also an open statement that my mission is steady improvement and an acknowledgement that I will never stop trying to improve at all that I do. Learning and improving are my "why."

In a presentation to fellow Brokers, I show a slide with two pictures: in the first is an X-ray of the human skull full of dollar signs with the caption "solutions for yourself," and in the second an X-ray of a human skull full of gears, its caption reads "solutions for your client." This is a vital distinction to make about your motivations. You will build a long-term viable business on clients that you solved problems for, not on commission checks. The people are the core, not the dollars. I have assisted clients with returning to their current lender, with plans that result in zero income. In fact, I have worked with clients whose transactions have cost me hundreds, sometimes thousands, to complete.

Focus on winning the client, not the commission.

As the professional in the equation, ensure that things end as you said they would from the start. Transactions must conclude for your clients exactly as the clients expected. One benefit to this business is that errors on the Broker's part

---

66 *Start with Why: How Great Leaders Inspire Everyone to Take Action* – Dec 27 2011 by Simon Sinek

are almost always of a financial nature and the Broker has a window of opportunity to make it right simply by writing a check, sometimes to the client, other times to the lawyer or the lender without the client even being aware that you did so. Fixing a problem quietly in the background, even one that costs you more than your commission to complete the file, is almost always the best way to handle a problem when possible.

When you tell a client about a problem, even one you are going to fix, or worse still, you go into the detail of what it is going to "cost you" to simply deliver what you said you would originally, you risk losing more than the commission, you risk losing the client.

Many things in this business can change or shift overnight: interest rates, policies, and procedures. Attempts to explain such shifts that have a negative impact on the client will only be met with frustration. Explanations accompanied by a story about how you are going to write the cheque to make it right are to be avoided at all times. Simply take care of the problem internally such that the client's experience is smooth from start to finish.

Always Do What You Say You Will Do

Do not make excuses, and do not go out of your way to paint a picture of yourself as the hero fixing a problem that a client simply will not understand the nature of.

An example is a recent mortgage commitment document from a lender that had an incorrect rate on it. I did not catch the missing 0.25% rate premium that was meant to be charged by the lender due to the unique program the file was approved under. The lender caught it after the client had already reviewed and signed the (incorrect) documents. The lender then wanted to issue a new commitment at the higher rate to be re-signed. I suggested to the lender that they do the math on their loss over the term of the mortgage and deduct the proceeds from my own compensation.

Going back to a client and saying "it's not my fault" was not an option I would accept. I had already committed to that client at the previous rate. Typo or not, the client would be less than impressed. Never worry about winning a specific commission, win the client.

Even more challenging for some Brokers than taking the hit for an external mistake is the next step you must take in that scenario. Silence. All too many of us want to receive credit for our suffering. It might even feel like you are passing up an opportunity to "look good," but silence is the best plan. I would prefer that a client think that no mistakes were made at all, rather than a mistake has been made for which I am paying the price. To try and explain the entire thing runs the risk of raising all too many other questions and creating greater concerns in the client's mind. What other errors has this lender made? How much is the Broker being paid that they can afford to absorb this cost? Etc.

To paraphrase John Wooden: the true test of a person's character is what they do when no one is watching.

When Things Go Really Wrong

When (not if) clients "break up" with you partway through a transaction, opting to return to their current lender, as often occurs with renewal and sometimes refinance transactions in the early days as you get your footing and master the business, it is important to never let on to the clients how truly soul-crushing this experience is. Do not react. Absorb the news and respond professionally. Never suggest to the clients that they "owe you" for a prepaid appraisal or for your planning expertise. It is vital to stay on the high road, always smiling, always helpful, always polite and letting the clients know that should things not work out with the other lender that you will be there for them, that you will keep the approval alive in the system, just in case. Thank them for being upfront with you; in fact, commend them for this.

You appreciate them, you appreciate the communication.

When travelling this difficult (but correct) path, you will be surprised at just how many clients return when the other lender fails to deliver. However clients will only return if the initial rejection was handled with maturity, with understanding (even when you do not understand at all) and with good-humoured disposition. That client must be left with a clear view that your office door remains wide open to them. If you react negatively they will not return no matter what happens; in fact, they may seek out another Broker right across the street from you just to avoid the discomfort.

A client's desire to avoid being seen as "wrong" is equally as powerful as yours may be to be seen as "right." Resist the urge to be "right" and simply be awesome!

Nobody wins in a world defined as "one is right and the other is wrong." Little in Brokering, as with life, is black and white; instead, it is mostly shades of grey tinted by varying degrees of clear communication.

The overriding goal with every file, with every opportunity, is to create raving fans. Even when it hurts badly, when you are feeling betrayed by a client with whom dozens of hours have been spent, with your own personal payments looming. Always opt for what is right for the client, be it asking a lender to reduce the compensation to make a file work, or advising a client on a product that pays you one third of the compensation of another, or suggesting a client delay their completion date by 45 or even 180 days because this works out better for them. Always side with the client's best interests. This never ceases to pay off exponentially.

Our services are not the answer for 100% of clients 100% of the time. Understanding this and being able to advise clients of an alternative solution, even a solution that puts not one thin dime into your pocket, is what will allow you to build a base of raving fans.

Sound advice delivered with integrity and honesty is the only path to creating raving fans.[67] And a base of raving fans is a wonderful way to build a business. It is perhaps the only way.

67   *Raving Fans: A Revolutionary Approach to Customer Service* – May 19 1993 by Kenneth
     H. Blanchard & Sheldon M. Bowles

CHAPTER 19

COMMUNICATE WITH INTENTION... AND THE TELEPHONE

Much of this chapter will focus on the ultimate productivity tool, the telephone. Few devices allow one to so efficiently build a relationship. For those who are sceptical of this method and demand that it is "all about the face-to-face meetings," I say, "Give me a call."

You already use the phone daily, but do you use it well? Enhanced telephone skills help everyone. Whether speaking with family, friends, booking a flight, disputing a bill, ordering a pizza...learning to build rapport within minutes allows you to both deliver and receive a much better experience.

Smile

When speaking with a client on the phone, you must sound

happy, even when you may not be. You must sound deeply interested in what the other person is saying. The more engaged you are, the more this radiates through the phone line. When engaged, you're more likely to control the flow of the conversation, which is important for efficiency. Digressing onto tangents about politics, the latest bank profits or the Illuminati is not moving the conversation forward. This is moving it sideways.

Count on the individual at the other end of the line being engaged, as this call is potentially about the largest transaction of their life. They will know if you're paying attention. Although they may not physically see you (Skype/FaceTime) glancing at text messages or email, scrolling through Facebook or Googling travel destinations, they will know. Those who are engaged sense when others are not.

Get up and walk around the office while on the phone. We all spend far too much time sitting behind a desk. Aside from the health benefits of simply standing and stretching regularly, walking and talking helps limit distractions (i.e., the computer) and maintains focus on the conversation at hand. I use over-the-ear Bose Bluetooth headphones with an excellent microphone built in for all calls. This gives me mobility, and keeps my hands free to type an application, or just wave my arms around expressively as I stand alone in my office.

Control the Flow

Every now and then I do get verbally steamrolled by a client. They need to talk themselves out. Eventually it will be my turn, in the meantime I listen and take notes until they wear themselves out. Again, if not taking notes, it's better to walk around to prevent yourself from tuning out because just when you think the monologue will never end, the client asks, "What do you think?" And you won't know what to think if you don't know what was said.

Few lapses in professional etiquette are more embarrassing than not having a response to a topic that a client has just unloaded 5,000 words on, especially if you're talking to this person for the first time. First impressions matter over the phone just as much as in person.

Voicemail

Do you answer calls on the first ring? If the call goes to voice-mail is your message professional, assuring the caller that messages will remain confidential? Do you say you'll call back promptly? I never place a client on hold, they have my undivided attention.

Updating your voicemail message every morning creates a good impression. "Good day, it's August 5th, this is the confidential voicemail of Dustan Woodhouse, please leave a message. I am in the office today and will return your call as quickly as possible. Thank you." Of course, that message can backfire if you're not actually in the office all day. You also risk sounding sloppy if you fail to update that message early each morning (or perhaps just before bed). If you miss a day though, you are effectively telling callers you're in the office August 5th, but now it's the 6th and they will be left to wonder whether you're working today. They may assume you have taken the day off and call another Broker. Whoops.

There are simple ways to make a good impression. Remember your manners, always saying, "May I?" "Please," and "Thank you." Don't reserve the niceties for clients. Be courteous to secretaries and other gatekeepers because they may relay the impression you made on them to their bosses, chances are that they too have a mortgage to discuss. The simplest path here is to just be polite at all times to all people. You cannot go wrong with this approach to life. It is like overdressing your personal demeanor. Being a man of few words and many explosions might work for the Hollywood action hero, but not so much for an aspiring Broker.

Start practicing active listening now.

Be Literate

The written word is a Brokers primary form of communication. It's excusable not to know how to use a semi-colon (I still don't), but misspelling words chips away at your credibility. Although it doesn't catch all errors, spell-checking your emails and other correspondence is a no-brainer. Brokering is a game of precision, precise numbers and precise wording of contracts and clauses, so correct spelling, grammar and sentences in basic communications gives clients the confidence in you and your ability to handle their transaction.

If you give a client one (however small) reason to doubt you, often nine more (equally small) will crop up. Rarely does a single lapse cause a file to implode. It's often a series of little lapses, death by a thousand cuts. I have seen client relationships, not just the transaction, deteriorate as small errors collect and form a large pile of doubt in a client's mind.

Poor communication has been at the root whenever a file has gone horrendously wrong; we are talking epic failures. I may only have made one single small error, which I failed to take ownership of and communicate clearly and quickly (that's two errors already). Then the compounding of additional circumstances, completely beyond my control, conspires to paint a picture so devastating that not only the transaction and the client are lost to me, but most devastating of all, the referral source is too. In the most extreme situation you may be losing a friend too. Mistakes in this business can be costly. Trying to build an analysis of where and how it all went wrong is something that your stressed-out clients have no time or inclination to pay any attention to. You are simply written off. Your referral source may cut you some slack, but keep in mind that you are now hurting their reputation as well.

When mistakes are made, own them quickly and own them thoroughly. Even the smallest ones.

Emails thanking people for referrals should go out instantly and should not be templates; they should be genuine. If you are using templates be very careful to update them with the name of the person you're emailing. It's embarrassing to thank John for his time today when John is actually Jane. I try to limit the use of templates, and the very few I use are written by me and are generic. No names.

An excellent program to filter any email templates through is 'Hemingway'. It highlights sentences that are unclear or too complex. Indeed I may have run this entire book through it had I discovered it sooner.

For people who know that their skills with speech and writing fall short of professional standards, ask for assistance. Take classes at a community college. A lack of confidence in writing can permeate communications. Resist telling yourself that enrolling in a class shows that you're dumb. It is the refusal to learn that is the dumb move. Education makes us masters of our domains.

Bad News

Always communicate news that's bad, slightly bad or even neutral by phone, if not in person. Never via email, let alone text. Clients are often quick to quit when problems arise. Talking problems through often leads to resolution. Rely on emails only when you're relaying good news, but then again, when it is good news, then you really want to call. How you handle tough situations often determines whether the client will retain you in the future and recommend you to others. Yes an email is easier when it comes to bad news; the phone call is way more difficult, and as it rings you pray for voicemail, but as always, the difficult path is the correct path.

If you get voicemail, just leave a basic message with your name and number only. Do not try and explain anything to a machine with a time limit on it.

Phoning with bad news isn't a rule everybody follows. Most people prefer to distance themselves with email. Keep this in mind the next time you are on the receiving end of an email containing (perceived) bad news; pick up the phone and call the sender. Or if you can't call immediately, reply with an email saying you're going to call as soon as you can. You will rise above others in your client's eyes as having some guts and integrity.

Talk things through—do not try to type them through.

Justified

If you're angry or upset and feel compelled to pound out something on your keyboard to explain how things "really are" keep in mind that the harder your fingers hit the keys, the less likely you should hit send. Don't hit "Reply," or worst of all "Reply All"; instead, hit "Forward" and type in your own email address. Sleep on what you sent to yourself. Read it again. Even if you've calmed down, softened your email and removed negative words, remember that an email doesn't reflect the tone of the sender. Email is taken in the tone of the recipient reading the words, it's where their head is that matters. In our family, when one of us is miffed at another, we often say, "That's a you-thing, not a me-thing." This thought applies to email. You might be typing something very witty or simply sarcastic, thinking you are hilarious. But if the recipient is in a less-than-perfect mood when they read it, things can go horribly wrong.

Ask yourself, why am I sending this barbed response, this

diatribe, this unsolicited scathing psychoanalysis? Perhaps you would do well to do what the sender of the email should have done in the first place: pick up the phone and talk it out. Be the bigger person.

Communicating with the Enemy

As counterintuitive as it may seem, I've been amazed at the benefits of communicating with the "enemy." There are synergies with competing lenders, even competing Brokers. Often, we can help each other out.

Early in 2009, while attending one of my first Real Estate Action Group meetings the host asked all the mortgage reps in the room to stand up and introduce themselves. I was one of three. Ironically enough in a room of 200 people sitting right next to me was a mobile mortgage specialist from one of the chartered banks. We had a laugh as we had each ostensibly attended in order to meet potential clients and instead wound up sitting next to the "enemy."

As we talked, we learned that we each had access to different products. We discovered additional opportunities when we met for lunch later, another example of follow-through and building an unlikely relationship. To this day we continue to refer clients to one other. We have never really kept precise track of who owes who what. We simply refer clients to the other that we ourselves cannot help. Each of us knows that the other will treat those clients with the utmost care. Each of us strives to make the other one look good in the eyes of the client.

This is another relationship that has resulted in several million dollars in mortgage transactions flowing back and forth between us over the years.

It is not just a matter of communicating well and communicating often, but also being open to communicating with those that others might discount. There is a take-away in nearly every single conversation you have, from one with a homeless person to one with a CEO and everybody in between.

The irony in this specific example is that I reached out to a mortgage representative of another bank only a few weeks before, their response was, "I see no benefit in spending my valuable lunch hour with a competing Broker." This was a rather narrow-minded viewpoint, one that has cost that person massively in missed opportunity.

Communicate clearly, communicate often and always be positive. Opportunity is lurking in the most unlikely places, but to discover it often requires a bit more conversation than most will engage in.

CHAPTER 20

IDENTIFY WITH YOUR CLIENTS

You can't relate to a superhero, to a superman, but you can identify with a real man who in times of crisis draws forth some extraordinary quality from within himself and triumphs but only after a struggle.

— TIMOTHY DALTON

What you've done in your life—success or failure, business or personal, is the foundation for making connections. As a Broker, one of the easiest starting points is your own personal mortgage experience. Take the time to write down the details of that experience, good and bad, and look for opportunities to make them a part of your story with clients. The challenges and the opportunities that were important to you during your own financing will resonate with your clients. Seize every opportunity to genuinely identify with your clients.

No Soup For You

One of the first questions in the mortgage software is date of birth. When clients are within a couple of years of my age I always make the comment, "Ah, perfect, we were born (nearly) the same year, my pop-culture references will work with you." Often this results in a quick 80's or 90's catchphrase.

If you're dealing with a first-time homebuyer, you will recall how foreign the experience was for you. Let them know that you too were nervous about all the same things. It doesn't matter whether you bought your first home a month ago or 30 years ago. The dynamics and emotions haven't changed. Give clients space and time to express their concerns and doubts. As with most things, you can never listen too much. And very likely you can assuage many of their concerns, but not if you are unaware of them.

The Trickier Part

You may be taking an application from a business owner wanting to leverage their property for reinvesting in his successful (or struggling) company. As Brokers, we don't judge whether the owner is making the right or wrong move. I do share my experiences as a business owner because I think my wins, just as much as my mistakes, may be useful to clients. The fact is that 94% of businesses fail within the first ten years. What this often means is that either you or your client have struggled in the past or are struggling currently. If you can offer constructive advice, not destructive commiseration, then do so. Don't hide your experience with hard times; tell those stories, especially when helping a client facing their own tough times. If you can say with honesty that you've been there, then say it.

As a previous business owner, you can also talk to business clients about slow-paying accounts, difficult employees, and hiring and firing. Even if you've never owned a business, you can share insights about where you have worked—small business or large corporation. We all have experiences that are relevant on some level. Stay relevant and on topic.

The Hard Part

Once I took a bit of a chance while talking with a struggling business owner. I asked him whether he spent a lot of nights sitting up until 3am, flipping channels aimlessly, not really feeling worthy of the house he lived in, perhaps not feeling worthy of anything in his life at all. Just staring into the abyss... There was a long pause, then he replied, "You really have been here. That's exactly what I'm doing."

Connection made.

I shared the titles of some books that helped get me through that stretch. On occasion I will courier a copy from the collection that I keep on a shelf in my office for exactly this sort of situation. When a client sitting in my office expresses an interest in a book on the shelves behind me, I pull a copy off my shelf, write a little note on the inside cover and tuck in one of my business cards as a bookmark.

When couriering a book, be aware of the conversation and the book title. It may be better sent to either the client's home or their office. You do not want to create an awkward situation for them in front of co-workers or staff. Yes, this is a strategic practice, but as you can likely tell by now, for me the giving of a book is a genuine gesture. There's nothing wrong with being strategic and genuine at the same time.

The Little Things

It is the little things that matter in life. The small gift that says we were thinking of one another. You will not build rapport with everyone that you come into contact with, but when the opportunity presents itself to make a genuine and meaningful connection please embrace it. Do not let it pass.

Recently, I ran into clients who two years ago sent me a unique thank-you gift. They both were into dirt biking, and knew that I was as well. They took the time to get a motocross jersey emblazoned with my name on the back. I wear that jersey only on fair-weather days, and think of them every time I do. They made the connection with me.

One of my referral sources mentioned that he was a huge Gordon Lightfoot fan; it came up in passing, but a year later when Gordon Lightfoot came to town I made a point of locking down front-row-centre tickets and that resonated with my referral source for some time. Pay attention, take notes and take action when the opportunity arises to do something special.

There are multiple layers to identifying with and making

connections with people. This is a people business. It is "personal selling" with 99% personal and 1% selling.

CHAPTER 21

REGISTER, WRITE, COMMIT

"The moment you take responsibility for everything in your life is the moment you can change anything in your life"

– HAL ELROD

Decision Time

If you are leaning even 51% towards making this move after reading this book:

Just do it!

Register!

At the very least you will have taken a definitive and meaningful step in your life. You still have months to make a final decision.

Take the exam!

Too many register for the course, without a plan, complete the assignments haphazardly, again without a plan, and then, realizing that failing to plan is planning to fail, get cold feet and never take the exam. Forcing them to re-register (pay fees a second time) and re-write all the modules. What a colossal waste of money, energy and, most important, time.

You committed the money, energy and time to reading this book, and for that I thank you.

You should have a much better idea of whether or not to commit the money, energy and time to completing the course and entering the field of Mortgage Brokering.

Afraid of failing? At some point every day, we all are. Every day I know I am, but every day I know I will learn something new that will make me just a little bit better than I was the day before. There is always something new and different happening. New and different are scary, and of course the amygdala says new + different = bad. And so we must run and hide from the new and the different to be safe.

NO!

This is a multiple-choice exam that we are talking about, not a sabre-toothed tiger. The exam cannot maul you, at least not physically. So take charge, and reread the passage at the start of this book on how to prep for the exam.

Commit. There is no try, there is only do or do not.[68]

---

68 Yoda

WHAT'S NEXT?

"At the end of the day, let there be no excuses, no explanations, no regrets."

— STEVE MARABOLI

You may have concluded that Brokering seems difficult (it is), and that the distinct possibility of a significant struggle during the first 6 to 18 months exists (it does). Such a career may not be the best fit for you. If so, this $20 book has saved you more than just the thousand-dollar course fee. It has bypassed the stress of the entire roller-coaster-like experience. An experience that drives between 85% and 95%, depending on territory, of new mortgage agents out of (the) business in less than two years.

Risking years of your life, years that could have been better invested in other activities, is not a decision to make lightly.

Either way I hope that you build a new contact card for every person who ever calls or emails you again. The adoption of this single habit, wherever life takes you, will have made this book worthwhile.

On the other hand, if you have decided that this is the path for you, then I look forward to meeting you again in Volume 2: *Your First One-Hundred Files.*[69]

Volume 2 is focused on files 1 through 100 as a brand-new Broker:

- The additional habits to form
- The tips and tricks of application software and processing
- Key strategies for building client and referral source relationships
- Choosing the right sources of business and avoiding the wrong ones

And, most important, running a client's file all the way across the finish line.

2008/2009, my first 12 months as a Broker, could be called 'the iceberg year'. On the surface, I was a shiny-happy top-producing Broker; closing files, achieving various milestones, outperforming industry expectations. All the while, few knew what lay beneath the surface of that facade. None of my colleagues understood my true financial situation at that time.

---

69 A working title at this time.

Each of us has our challenges at various times, it is how we weather them that defines our character.

The prospect of extricating myself from that financial predicament spurred me to jump into the business with both feet and not look back. Within a week of earning my Broker's license, I left the security of a steady paycheque, a company car, and extended healthcare benefits. I departed with no severance package, no safety net, just lots of debt.

In Volume 2 we will address the topic of when, and most importantly how, to leave your job smoothly.

One of many valuable lessons learned over years of working with hundreds of clients is that most of us, were we brought a list of our own personal challenges on paper and told that the list belongs to another person, could in short order develop a simple solution for this "other" person's problems.

We are excellent at solving the problems of others. Yet somehow fail to apply our own advice to our own lives. The clearest personal judgment arrives in the moments of repression of this flawed thought pattern. When we hear, and heed, the words of our own advice things really do improve. So listen to the advice of others, and write out your own challenges and aspirations and give them as objective a look as you can.

It was this realization, born from preparing presentations on Brokering, which led me to write this series of books, a series that is as much about the Broker I am today as it is the Broker I will be tomorrow.

Volume 2 will include case studies of several of my first 50 clients. Focusing on the origins of the clients, and the lending solutions found for them. In some cases other Brokers had already advised the clients that there was "no hope."

There will be greater detail on what converts clients into referral sources and/or repeat clients. You will handle your first 50 clients better than I handled mine. You will formulate a business plan and stick to it. You will learn to seek out and work with mentors and coaches, to efficiently and effectively master social media and other technologies. I will share scripts for locking down complete applications on opening phone calls, and scripts for smoothly completing the closing document packages. I will reinforce the message that your outlook on life drives, or stalls, your business.

I want to build your enthusiasm for the business, tempered with an understanding of what you're getting into. This business is difficult, demanding and complicated. It's also fulfilling and rewarding in that you are given opportunities to truly help people. And yes, it can be lucrative too. That's the beauty of becoming a licensed Mortgage Broker; it offers the total package of fulfillment and reward for effort. You can shape it into the business you want, and you can stake out a comfortable spot or keep on climbing higher.

It is my sincere hope that we will meet again in Volume 2. We will pick up on your first day as a newly licensed Broker and give you a fresh collection of core principles to put into practice. We will build upon all that has been discussed thus far and enhance it in order to launch your new business quickly while simultaneously building a lasting foundation.

The early days require a deft mix of both hunter and farmer skills. Picture a farmer on a tractor planting seeds for tomorrow, but with a rifle slung over his (or her) shoulder to provide food for tonight. Hold this thought. After Volume 2, this will be you.

> *"There is no happiness except in the realization that we have accomplished something."*
>
> — HENRY FORD

VOLUME 2: PREVIEW

My First File

How a nightmare file combined with a nightmare golf game landed me a dream client.

Looking back now, my first file was the stuff of nightmares for a seasoned Broker. But I was too new, and way too optimistic, to see it for the challenge it was.

It was a seven-figure file closing in two weeks. The client had placed a $500,000 deposit, had no subjects in the offer (meaning no way out), and was self-employed with an accordingly low documented income (meaning limited lending options).

"Can you get it done?" he asked.

"Not a problem," I replied coolly.

I practically ran down the hall Monday morning to see my manager, who in turn advised me that "this deal will not close on time, if it closes at all." Then having a second thought she suggested I call a specific lender rep that I'd met only a few days earlier.

Of the many lessons I learned with that first file, the most important are related to relationships. Relationships saved my butt, and continue to do so to this day.

Relationships From the Past

Before I became a Broker, I'd been a founding partner in a company within an entirely different industry. Since selling that company I had made an effort to meet at least one former client per week for lunch, dinner or even just coffee. There was no master plan at the time; it just seemed prudent to stay in touch. The fact was I had friendships of some degree with many of these people, having done business for ten to fifteen years. I enjoyed speaking with them about their business, and I enjoyed sending them clients when I could.

Keeping these relationships intact was to pay unexpected dividends during my first week as a Broker, when a call came asking if I was officially licensed yet. The caller was a gentleman with whom I had seven years of previous business dealings. There was a long history of trust between us.

Then he presented me with the aforementioned "challenging" scenario.

How did this file get approved and closed on time? The same way any complicated rush file does to this day: through a quality relationship with a lender representative.

Relationships of the Future

As a first-week Broker, I didn't really know any lender representatives, although a few days earlier I had attended an industry golf tournament, despite having golfed maybe twice in my life. All day my "skills," or lack thereof, were scrutinized and much lamented by my teammates. Nonetheless, I had set aside my fear of potential (OK inevitable) embarrassment and shown up in order to meet the industry players. And if I hadn't, if instead I had let fears of ridicule hold me back, the very course of my business would have been altered significantly.

A new friend, a lender representative, whom I met on the course, helped to shepherd my first client's file through the system—amongst hundreds of files she was overseeing—she took the time to coach me along the way. This help stemmed from one happenstance meeting at an event I was reluctant to even attend.

The net result was a very happy client who promptly requested that I refinance another of his properties, and shortly thereafter the proceeds from that transaction led to yet another purchase for him.

My first client represented not only 25% of the transactions during the first six months of my practice, he also represented 45% of the mortgage volume, and thus 45% of the income generated during the same period. He was, and remains, very important to my business.

Relationships Today

During a recent conversation, seven years nearly to the day later, client #1 told me he in fact had no plan B in place on that first file, I was his Plan A, B & C. He had complete faith I would make it happen. Luckily, I did as well.

What of the lender relationship that began with a nightmarish round of golf and this subsequent transaction?

As with the client, the lender rep and the lender continue to play a key role in my business, with as much as ~40% of my annual volume flowing to that lender to this day. The lessons learned on that very first file led me to submit additional files to them from which I, in turn, learned additional lessons. The collection of "secrets"[70] that I have amassed on how files are truly underwritten and approved is large and constantly evolving.

All relationships are built on trust. The first lesson is to build trust on a variety of levels with everyone you know. Build that trust early and build it often. Trust takes time. In this career,

---

70 Secrets? i.e. if you leave the employment fields blank, or delete them completely for the co-applicant due to said co-applicant being a homemaker or retired this (the blank/missing fields) will cause the file submitted to bypass the APV (automated property valuator) triggering an instant request for an appraisal. I learned this around file #1020. Conclusion; I have spent thousands on appraisals needlessly simply because I was unaware of this system foible. I guarantee Brokers with ten years experience are reading this and uttering the words "no way." Such is this business.

time starts out feeling like your worst enemy and then grows into your best friend. With 85%+ of the mortgage agents you started out with gone in less than two years, you stand out as more familiar simply by lasting those first few years. You are also, at that point in time, on the cusp of your first-year's clients starting to hit the average early refinance date, six in ten clients will break their mortgage early, at an average of 38 months in. This gives you yet another opportunity to build trust.

With time, your established referral sources, and seeds planted years earlier with past and potential clients starting to bring in a steady harvest, it does become easier. Or at least the challenges themselves become ones that you had always wished for (too much business). Be careful what you wish for.

Admittedly, in the early days, time feels more like your enemy. Planting seeds that you cannot harvest for a few years is not helping you pay the bills this month, and can be frustrating. But staying the course, and staying calm, is integral to building long-term success while keeping an eye open for immediate opportunities.

As it turns out, I had been planting seeds of trust for years prior to entering the business, not as any sort of master plan, but simply by doing the right thing by people when the opportunity arose. It is never too late to start.

ABOUT THE AUTHOR

In a field of 18,000 Brokers, Dustan Woodhouse has ranked in the top 20, by production, for 6 years running as recorded by Canadian Mortgage Professional (CMP Top 75).

In the Spring of 2017 Dustan was awarded one of the industry's highest honours—"Broker of the Year" at the Canadian Mortgage Awards gala.

Dustan originally entered the world of Mortgage Brokering from a completely unrelated field (high performance car tuning). With no financial services background per se he hit the ground running, and in his first calendar year was the #1 individual Broker in his firm. With a relentless work ethic and a desire to constantly improve, Dustan climbed the ranks of the industry, and in his sixth year exceeded $100 million in annual volume, and has maintained that level since.

Dustan lives in Vancouver with his wife and two children. When not in his office, he can be found racing through the trees on a dirt bike or downhill mountain bike making the most of the local mountain trails.

Volume 2

A MUST BUY FOR ANYONE IN THE CANADIAN MORTGAGE FIELD
By Nick Bachusky on October 7, 2016

Once again another gift to my favourite industry in Canada, the mortgage industry. I used to call him the Wayne Gretzky of the mortgage industry but after consideration I have to change that to I don't know what. The reason being that Wayne Gretzky was the greatest player but not a very good coach because he could not relate to players with less talent whereas Dustan is both.

He lays out a winning game plan that will allow any newbie (or veteran stuck in a rut) a clear path to achieving effective results full of integrity. He makes it clear that it is not an easy road, nor a get rich quick scheme, but a path that is going to be challenging but rewarding if followed. Your clients will benefit, you will benefit, your referral partners will benefit and your family will benefit. Win-Win-Win-Win.

If you are new to this industry or continually love to grow in this great profession it is easily a must read.

THE OWNER'S MANUAL FOR YOUR MORTGAGE BUSINESS

By Amazon Customer on October 18, 2016

★ ★ ★ ★ ★

Dustan, thank you for making the time to put together the "Be The Better Broker" series. Volume 2 is a roadmap to kick-starting a mortgage business. This book is engaging, to the point, and filled with valuable information. Anyone who is a Mortgage Broker, or wants to be a Mortgage Broker, needs to read this book. I also thought many times that this book would apply to almost anyone with entrepreneurial aspirations. I heard it described as the CliffsNotes for Mortgage Brokering, and it definitely is. Dustan has dedicated his time to learn the ins and outs of building a successful mortgage business, and this book puts you on the fastest path to learn how to do the same. I have already successfully implemented a few of the methods Dustan outlines; one method is how he takes an application (such a time saver and borrowers are happy with how simple it makes the process), and the A-Z script has been a great tool to have in my back pocket. I look forward to continuing my education, from Dustan, when Volume 3 is released.

EVEN BETTER THAN THE FIRST

By Andrew Hendrie on March 15, 2017

★ ★ ★ ★ ★

Even better than the first book. Great for anyone who's recently completed the mortgage agent licensing course. Can't wait for volume 3 to come out in Kindle format so I can finish the series.

ESSENTIAL READING FOR ANYONE IN THE MORTGAGE INDUSTRY

By Manson R Parks on October 6, 2016

This book should be mandatory reading as part of the certification process for mortgage brokers. The level of practical details for someone thinking of entering the industry is truly remarkable. I found it refreshing to read a book that isn't afraid to actually recommend something. For example, rather than saying "Go find some clients, how you do this will vary for everyone" this book gives practical examples of how others have found clients so the reader can contemplate which style would work best for them. Even advice on systems related topics, such as apps or services that a new broker might find useful, is dispensed with examples of what has worked for Dustan

Ultimately this book is balanced look at what it takes to be successful in this industry delivered in a way that is encouraging yet not sugarcoated. I read volume one and two in less than a week because the content was accessible (clear, concise, with an enjoyable flow-and some humour), informative and engaging

I recommend this book for anyone thinking of entering the industry or anyone already in the industry. Even if you are successful you can always learn more and take your business further.

Great job Dustan!

YOU NEED THIS BOOK!

By Scott B on October 5, 2016

This is a must have book! Not just for the new broker but for anyone in the business. I have been a broker for 11 years and there is still much to learn. Learning from one of the best in the business is a great way to start or continue your growth. My book is marked up and highlighted like I have owned it for years. I have had it for 1 week. I just finished the book and I am about to restart it again. Do yourself a favor and pick up both of the Volumes that are available now. I am sure the next 2 are going to be just as good or better. Well done Dustan!

EXCELLENT READ.

By Cory Vanceon September 16, 2016

Once again Dustan is able to deconstruct the business of Mortgage Brokering and provide a road map to success. The title easily could have been the Road Map to $100 million. Don't let the sub title fool you this should be read by anyone who wants to improve no matter how long they have been in the industry. This book is filled with tactical tips that anyone can use and start using immediately. Finally, this can be used as a guide for success in other industries by simply removing the mortgage brokering references. Looking forward to Volume 3.

A MUST READ!

By Ryan Oakeon September 16, 2016

If you work in the mortgage industry, you need to read this. I am fortunate enough to be within my first 100 days of working full time as an independent broker and having this book as a road map to success is beyond satisfying. I can't think of a better role model to use as a benchmark to what I need to be doing in this complex industry. Volume 2 is like having an answer key to a test, I cannot wait to model my business around Dustan's stories and advice. Thank you Dustan!

AWESOME JOB DUSTAN

By Patricia Mckeanon September 27, 2016

★ ★ ★ ★ ★

Hello Dustan I just wanted to write you and thank you for the great book Be The Better Broker Volume 2. I just finished it and I enjoyed it immensely. It reminded me of lot of things I should and could be doing better after 13 years licensed. I think both of your books should be mandatory for every new mortgage associate to read as it really teaches you important information that the mandatory courses do not. Great job!

... AGAIN WITH HIS VOLUME 2 OF THE BE THE BETTER BROKER SERIES

By Michael Atkinson on September 11, 2016

★ ★ ★ ★ ★

Dustan amazes us again with his Volume 2 of the Be the better broker series. For anyone looking to enter the Mortgage Broker industry, or even if you are 2+ years into the industry, this is a must read. Dustan puts into writing the essentials of running your own business and how to win and retain clients.

INSIGHTFUL. REFRESHINGLY HONEST. HIGHLY RECOMMEND.

By Trish on December 15, 2016

★ ★ ★ ★ ★

Excellent, straight to the point advice from an industry pro. I can't wait to read volumes 3 and 4. If you are just starting out as an agent or broker or looking to jump start your business, this is a must read series.

Volume 3

MORE .... GIVE ME MORE WORDS.

By Brad Lockey on March 15, 2017

★ ★ ★ ★ ★

Volume 4 can't come soon enough.

MUST HAVE FOR ANY NEW OR VETERAN BROKER

By Harold on December 30, 2016

★ ★ ★ ★ ★

Thanks to Dustan's poise, professionalism and integrity, he's opened his office door for others in the industry to learn from his habits, mistakes and triumphs. Dustan definitely lives the adage that "Brokering should be collaborative, not competitive". A nuts and bolts collection of processes, scripts and hardcore insight into the day-in-the-life of a successful mortgage broker. His insights and recommendations are useful not only within the mortgage broker industry, but all professional industries that value outstanding customer service, integrity and professionalism. I have a good understanding of just how busy Dustan's office is, and so I'm even more in awe that he was actually able to fund the time and ambition to create and publish this outstanding work. To your continued success Dustan!

LIKE PRINGLES, ONCE YOU POP YOU CAN'T STOP
By Manson R Parks on December 9, 2016
★ ★ ★ ★ ★

We know that you don't get something for nothing but this book comes close to proving that point wrong. The price of this book is a pittance compared to the years of hard work that Dustan has put in to be able to write a book like this. Buying this book gives you access to the tools and techniques that he has used to make himself one of the most successful mortgage brokers within Canada. This is not a "do this and you will be millionaire" type of book but it is evident after just a few chapters that if you do take his advice you can spare yourself many headaches and hassles as you grow your business. I am a new broker so I have found it inspiring and instructional. However, I believe that any broker (regardless of experience) would benefit from reading this.

Outstanding contribution Dustan!

CHRISTMAS HAS COME EARLY.
By Cory Vanceon December 15, 2016
★ ★ ★ ★ ★

Dustan continues to add immense value to our industry. There is no doubt he has been able to level up everyone else's game over the past 12 months with his series. This book is truly outstanding and packed with actionable tactics that will help you "Be Better". He could charge 10 times the price for what you will get in this edition.

If this book does not help you avoid having to do one full appraisal, save one client from going to their own bank, or get one more file completed then nothing will. This book will continue to sit on the desk to be reviewed each month.

Thank you for all you do for our industry.

LIKE A WISE FRIEND OR A KIND TEACHER
By Suzanne Fleur de Lys - Aujla on November 25, 2016
★ ★ ★ ★ ★

Reading is an essential component of development. Like a wise friend or a kind teacher, Dustan Woodhouse – educator, mentor and mortgage broker- walks you through a complete, easy to follow "How to Guide" on building business but also best practices. Dustan's personal success is not only the best review but also his kindness and support he gives to the Mortgage Broker Community. I Challenge you not only to do the work laid out in his book but also I challenge you to do it with as much grace as Dustan. #beabetterbroker #bebetter

YOU WILL BE A BETTER BROKER!!
By Earl Smithon November 27, 2016
★ ★ ★ ★ ★

What can I say, Dustan will enhance the business of any Broker who takes to read and implement practises from this great book. The entire series of books are easy to read and straight to the point. Best practises abound in this 3rd volume. I know I am a better Broker already for having read these books.

TOTALLY AWESOME BOOK!

By Amazon Customer on January 4, 2017

★ ★ ★ ★ ★

The Mortgage Bible Plain and Simple! Buy it! You will thank Dustan later!

WELL SAID WELL WRITTEN WELL DONE

By Rose McIntosh on January 7, 2017

★ ★ ★ ★ ★

A must read for everyone that handles Mortgages !!!!!!!!

THEY KEEP GETTING BETTER AND BTBB V3 WILL NOT DISAPPOINT

By Michael Hallett on November 25, 2016

★ ★ ★ ★ ★

wow, another blockbuster. DW has hit-it-out-of-the-park yet again. They keep getting better and BTBB V3 will not disappoint. There are so many gold nuggets that you just don't know where to start. There is a flow, so try and do your best to stay in the chapter sequence. Whether you are a 20 year veteran or fresh from graduating from the broker course there is something for everyone. Buy the book - buy the series! If you are a mortgage broker BTBB V3 is a must.